Instant Relaxation

How To Reduce Stress At Work, At Home And In Your Daily Life

State-Of-The-Art Fun And Easy Exercises
For Developing The Advanced Ability Of
Flying Into A Calm

Debra Lederer
and
Michael Hall, Ph.D.

Crown House Publishing Limited

First published by
Crown House Publishing Ltd
Crown Buildings
Bancyfelin, Carmarthen, Wales, SA33 5ND, UK
www.crownhouse.co.uk
and

Crown House Publishing Company, LLC
6 Trowbridge Drive, Ste. 5, Bethel, CT 06801, USA
www.crownhousepublishing.com

© Debra Lederer & Michael Hall, Ph.D., 1999, 2000

First published in 1999, and reprinted in 2000, 2004, 2006, and 2007.

The right of Debra Lederer and Michael Hall to be identified as the authors of this work has been asserted by them in accordance with the Copyright, Designs and Patents Act of 1988.

British Library Catalouging-in-Publications Data
A catalog entry for this book is available
from the British Library.

13 digit ISBN: 9781899836369
10 digit ISBN: 1899836365

LCCN 2004116487

Printed in the United States of America

About The Authors

Debra Lederer earned a bachelor's degree in psychology from the University of Michigan. She is a certified yoga instructor from the 3HO Foundation. Over the past ten years, she has given stress reduction workshops to numerous companies and organizations and has built a successful consulting practice in New York City. Debra has also trained as a Master Practitioner of NLP.

Debra Lederer
Health Works
422 E. 72nd St, Suite 15D
New York
NY 10021
USA
(212) 714-8128
www.balancedyoga.com

Michael Hall has graduate degrees in clinical psychology and Cognitive Behavioral psychology and psycholinguistics. After spending years as an LPC in private practice in Colorado, Michael has written more than a dozen books, *The Secrets of Magic, Meta-States, Dragon Slaying, NLP: Going Meta* and several with Dr Robert Bodenhamer, *Figuring Out People, Mind-Lines* and *Time-Lining*. Dr Hall now travels and trains internationally presenting NLP and Meta-State Training.

Michael Hall
Institute of Neuro-Semantics
P.O. Box 9231
Grand Junction
CO 81501
USA
(970) 523-7877
nlpmetastates@onlinecol.com

Table Of Contents

Acknowledgements

There are several people I would like to acknowledge and express my gratitude to for significantly contributing to this book.

I would like to thank all of my spiritual teachers who have encouraged and helped me to understand my true nature. I met various teachers in India whose teachings had a direct influence on me. Many thanks to Osho, Gangagi, Poonjaji and to all the seekers I met on my path. While in Thailand, I spent a great deal of time at a monastery called Wat Po on the island of Koh Phanghan. I would like to thank Steve and Rosemary for their teachings of Buddhist meditations. I am also grateful for my yoga teachers who have shared their knowledge of timeless spiritual principles. There have been many, and a special acknowledgement to Madhava Daddario Ravi Singh and the Sivananda Yoga Center of New York and San Francisco.

I thank Richard Bandler and John Grinder for their knowledge and insights in the development of NLP, which serves as the basis of so much of the contents of this book. I also thank all of my NLP teachers in New York City—Steven Leeds, Kevin Creedon, Mary Vanderwart; and my NLP teachers in Santa Cruz—Robert Dilts and Judith DeLozier.

I am grateful to my parents and friends, especially Gary Dear and Evi Krasnow, who were encouraging and supportive while I wrote this book on stress reduction techniques. A special thanks to Ginny Dustin for her help with the graphic design illustrations and the cover design.

I thank the publishers, the visionary team at Crown House Publishing Ltd, for seeing the value in this project. Most of all, I express my gratitude to Michael Hall for his expertise in co-writing this book. His contribution has been overwhelming and immense.

Debra Lederer

New York City,
New York
January 2000

Foreword

After finishing college, my goal was to study meditation and relaxation techniques, while simultaneously traveling the world. In following my desire to learn from the best teachers around the globe, between jobs, I visited seventy countries on six continents. Depending on the country, I absorbed myself in different ways into the culture and studied their relaxation techniques. I noticed that many teachers used relaxation techniques that were developed hundreds of years ago. Many of the programs I participated in required extensive training, sitting in uncomfortable positions for long periods of times, chanting various mantras, and following certain religious philosophies. These earlier techniques worked for societies with more time on their hands. While I found these techniques effective, I did not find them practical for the fast-paced environment of the modern office and our busy lifestyles.

Today, our lifestyle requires that we move quickly. It requires that we employ coping techniques while staying centered during stressful situations. During my travels, I learned that we cannot control the world around us, but that we can control our reaction to events. For these reasons, I have formulated these highly effective, simple, fast and easy methods of relaxation. In this particular format, you learn how to actually fly into a powerful and resourceful state of calm. Once you learn the process, and begin to habituate it, you can then truly **experience instant relaxation.**

New York City,
New York
January 2000

Preface

I first met Debra at a *Meta-states Training* in New York City and immediately recognised both her special expertise in the area of relaxation, and her passion for it. She knew all about the ins-and-outs of relaxation—what it looked like, sounded like, felt like, etc. And in terms of State management (the subject of the Meta-states training), she really knew how to access her own state of inner calm that allowed her to stay focused and clear. She also knew how to coach others into the same experience.

The area of mutual interest—NLP and State management—lead us to begin collaborating about a book. In the months that followed, Debra provided me with an entire manuscript on the subject. In fact, for the most part, you have that manuscript in the following pages. Through our talking and e-mailing, we decided to title it **Instant Relaxation.**

In the following pages, I have added some explanation sections and some touches here and there to the training of Stress Management that Debra has studied and presented over the past ten years with businesses and in personal consultations. You will find a work that explains, shows and coaches you how to develop your own ability to *"Fly Into a Calm"* anywhere and anytime you choose.

Debra wrote an entire text before I ever got involved. Her exercises and ideas on the *Relaxed Core State* arose from the actual hands-on experience of coaching clients through the process of relaxation in the context of their daily stresses. Her skill truly lies in the development of these exercises. Now you can also receive her coaching as you read and practice. Doing this program will enable you to easily learn to access states of inner calm and peace.

I became involved in this out of my strong belief in State management, and in using the neuro-linguistics approach (NLP) to access our most empowering states. The *neuro* part refers to using our neurology to its fullest potential. You will find that being aware of your breath and posture affects your state tremendously. *Linguistics* refers to our use of language and the languages of the mind to powerfully effect our states.

So now, through Debra's years of study and practice, you receive the benefit of the following direct, simple, and easy-to-follow step-by-step instructions. This means that you have in your hands a truly hands-on, *how-to-do-it* book. So as you read, you can just allow yourself to go ahead and fully experience the steps that will take you into this most resourceful state and when you get done, you will be able to demonstrate the power of **Flying Into A Calm.**

Michael

Michael Hall, Ph.D.
Grand Junction,
Colorado
January, 2000

part 1

intro
duction

Chapter One

Introduction

The Vision: Seven Days to Develop the Skills for Instant Relaxation

Do you find that time often becomes a source of stress for you? Do you find yourself under the pressure of deadlines? Do you find yourself running from one activity to the next? If you answered yes to these questions, this book offers you lots of solutions and ideas about controlling your state as you rush to complete your busy schedules and daily activities. Having stress and lots of responsibility in our lives is part of our modern lifestyle. Since we have such little time to complete all of our daily tasks and lists, having stress reduction exercises and coping skills becomes an essential part of remaining healthy and balanced in our life.

A major source of stress comes from "squeezing everything in" and having such little time to operate this way. Many people around the world spend much of their work day, sitting in an office and thinking about all the work they have to complete each day. Often, their thoughts travel to all of the plans and responsibilities outside of the office. Feeling stressed is a by-product of the job most people are not adequately paid for.

For these reasons, I have developed simple, short, innovative and powerful methods for stress reduction and relaxation. These transformational methods help you to "fly into a powerful and resourceful state of calm," both in your office and in whatever environment you choose. Once you understand and learn the process, it becomes a habit. Then you can have fun and use these methods for relaxation in an instant—anywhere and anytime.

These **Instant Relaxation Exercises** keep you calm, centered, energized, focused, and at ease as you complete your daily activities. If you invest just twenty minutes per day (ten minutes in the morning and ten minutes in the evening) over the next seven days, you will learn *the secrets of how to relax instantaneously*. Then, after those initial seven days, if you continue setting aside ten minutes each day (five minutes in the morning and five minutes in the evening) to feel your Relaxed Core State, you will feel refreshed and renewed. You will also feel empowered in the realization that you can re-access that state of *instant relaxation* whenever you desire.

The methods for the Instant Relaxation Exercises include the resources of breath techniques, postural alignment, focusing techniques, affirmations, and visualizations. We have put together a compilation of powerful and transformational relaxation techniques, tools and strategies. We have based this book upon the mnemonic—

Be Prepared For A Very Positive Aware Life.

This mnemonic stands for the exercises in this book: **B**reath, **P**osture, **F**ocus, **A**ffirmations, **V**isualizations, **P**attern Interrupts, **A**nchors and **L**anguage. Doing these exercises allows you to feel calm, centered, energized, focused, and at ease anywhere and anytime.

- We have based the tools, strategies and techniques that help you to instantly relax on a combination of physical and mental training.
- Physically, you focus on posture, breathing and movement exercises.
- Mentally, you work on focusing your mind through visualizations and affirmations. You will find that we have intentionally designed the Instant Relaxation Exercises in short and easy formats. Most exercises take less than five minutes and you practice them at any time and in any place.

Nuts and Bolts of the Process (The Relaxed Core State)

By practicing Instant Relaxation Exercises, you become increasingly in touch with your **Relaxed Core State.** This state of being centered within yourself is an ever-present part of you. Stepping into this state, you will feel calm, energized, focused, centered, at ease, and relaxed. **Relaxation signals,** such as your posture, breathing pattern, and choice of language will indicate that you have stepped into your Relaxed Core State.

As you continually practice Instant Relaxation Exercises, your mind will become focused, aware, and centered. And when your mind becomes focused, you will feel calmer, energized, focused, and at ease. You will find many different techniques and strategies which will leave you feeling great during your day. And the more aware you become of your physiology, thought and belief systems, the more control you will develop over your Relaxed Core State. Many people practicing Instant Relaxation Exercises feel more loving towards themselves, their family and others in their life.

Perhaps you have situations in your life that create tension and leave you feeling less empowered and confident. By following the guidelines laid out in this book, you will soon discover how you can stay calm and relaxed during these situations. My (D.L.) clients always feel amazed at how concentrating on their internal resources of breath, posture, focusing techniques, affirmations, and visualizations enhance their ability to feel good.

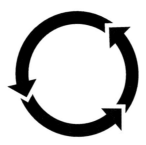

The Possibility of Instant Relaxation

You may wonder, "Can I actually change my state of mind and body so quickly?" I often hear people asking this question. Most people find it hard to shift out of a depressed or sad mood. How about you? Do you find that difficult? How about when you feel playful and happy? Do you find this a state that you enjoy staying in and experiencing?

We *break state* when interruptions and "pattern interrupts" shift us out of them. Take a moment to remember a time when you felt great and someone came to you with depressing news. Did that switch your state? How about when you felt bad and someone gave you great news? How about an experience where you felt relaxed and someone disrupted your calm state? What did they say or do to interrupt your state of inner calm? Assuming that you have vivid memories of shifting states, the following Instant Relaxation Exercises use this same principle.

Knowing that you have the knowledge and the ability to change states quickly becomes a valuable tool and resource for you. Changing the speed and pace of your breath, shifting elements of your posture, using focusing techniques, repeating affirmations, and visualizing describe internal resources that you can use to switch you into your Relaxed Core State.

How long will it take to access your Relaxed Core State?

Actually, you can start to reach your Relaxed Core State today. As you practice these quick, simple and fun exercises, notice how quickly you shift into your relaxed core state. After the first day, you should start discovering the part of yourself which feels calm, centered, energetic, focused and at ease. As each day passes, you will feel your Relaxed Core State growing stronger. And you will also learn how to step into this part of yourself faster.

When you make a commitment to practice the Instant Relaxation Exercises for one week (i.e. our seven-day program) your body and mind are trained to access your relaxed core state instantaneously. Do these exercises at your own pace and feel the soothing, calming effects of these exercises. Read one chapter a day for one week and practice the exercises at the end of each chapter. Spend about twenty minutes practising the exercises from each chapter (ten minutes in the morning and ten minutes in the evening). Select your favorite relaxation exercise from each chapter.

After the first week, continue practicing these instant relaxation techniques, ten minutes per day (five minutes in the morning and five minutes in the evening). Simply practice one exercise from each category. The categories include breath, posture, focusing exercises, affirmations, visualizations, pattern interrupts, anchors and language. At the end of this second week, you should be able to anchor your Relaxed Core State whenever you desire. I have broken the exercises down into short, quick and easy steps. These exercises provide all the tools, techniques and strategies you need to reach your Relaxed Core State.

The categories:
- Day 1:   Breath Exercises
           Breath Walking Exercises
- Day 2:   Posture Exercises
           Posture Check (Sitting and Standing)
- Day 3:   Focusing Exercises
           Eye Movements
- Day 4:   Affirmations
- Day 5:   Visualizations
- Day 6:   Pattern Interrupts
           Anchoring
- Day 7:   Language of Relaxation

Remember these exercises with the mnemonic:

Be Prepared For A Very Positive Aware Life
**(Breath, Posture, Focus, Affirmations, Visualizations
Pattern Interrupts, Anchors and Language)**

This mnemonic will help you to feel calm, centered, energized, focused, and at ease anywhere and at any time. So, turn the page, and let's begin Day One of the training!

part 2

seven
days
to
instant
relaxation

Chapter Two

Seven Days to Instant Relaxation

Day One: The Breath of Relaxation

Breath Exercises

Do you frequently or typically find yourself feeling sleepy after a few hours at the office? If so, your breathing pattern may explain why. If you take shallow breaths, your body will have a difficult time staying awake. But, change your breathing pattern and you will create different feelings in your body. As you breathe deeply from your abdomen, you will discover that your body feels energized and invigorated. On the next page we have listed two different breathing exercises. Each exercise gives you an example of how your breathing affects your energy level. You can do the following exercises while sitting or standing and practice the technique with your eyes open or closed.

Breath Refresher

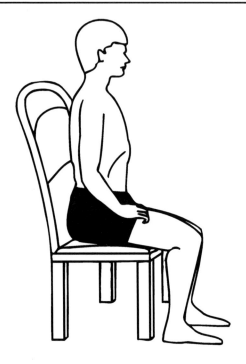

1. Focus on your nose and feel your breath.

2. Slowly count to 5 as you inhale a long, slow, deep breath through your nose.

3. Hold your breath for a count of 5.
   Silently say to yourself:
   1 long inhale
   2 long inhale
   3 long inhale
   4 long inhale
   5 long inhale.

4. After five seconds, slowly exhale through your nose to a count of 5.

5. Repeat this sequence ten times.

Aim to become aware of the sensations in your body. As you do, notice how you feel. Do you feel calmer? The more times you repeat this exercise, notice how much calmer, centered, energized and focused you feel. Continue to practice this sequence when you have a few spare minutes.

- Are you aware of any changes in your energy level?
- Do you feel drained after a few hours at the office?
- Do you start to feel stressed because your boss just added ten more items to your "in" basket?

Practice the breath refresher exercise

Notice how different you feel. Just a few minutes of deep breathing tremendously elevates your mood. Remember to practice this breathing technique anywhere and at any time.

A client, Amy, came to me (D.L.) reporting that she had a hard time staying awake at the office. She works as an accountant and explained that sitting at her desk for more than three hours causes her to yawn and to feel really tired. Amy practiced the exercises with me until she felt energized. She then decided to practice the exercises at her office.

Now, whenever she begins to feel tired, she does the breath refresher exercise. Amy told me that becoming aware of her breathing has made her more effective and productive at her job.

During the next exercise, you will practice breathing from your abdomen. Bringing your attention to your abdomen and breathing from this area allows both your chest cavity and lungs to fill with more oxygen. This creates a feeling of relaxation. You can do the following exercise while sitting or standing.

Breath Abdomen Refresher

1. Picture your abdomen and concentrate on your breath.
   Place either hand on your abdomen and slowly count to 5 as
   you inhale a long, slow and deep breath through your nose.

2. As you inhale a long, slow, deep breath, push your abdomen
   out.
   Picture a balloon being filled up with air

3. Hold your breath for a count of 5.
   Silently say to yourself:
   1 long inhale
   2 long inhale
   3 long inhale
   4 long inhale
   5 long inhale.

4. Now, exhale slowly through your nose to a count of 5. As you exhale, slowly pull your abdomen in. Picture a balloon being deflated.

5. Repeat this sequence ten times.

During the day, when you have a few minutes, practice this sequence of breathing. If you sit at your desk and feel tired, take a few minutes to practice abdomen breathing. Or, take a five-minute break, and practice abdomen breathing while walking to the rest room. Just a few minutes of deep breathing can tremendously elevate your mood. Remember to practice this breathing technique anywhere and at any time. You can practice this technique with your eyes open or closed.

Joe works as a media planner and came to my office complaining that his stomach hurt around 10 a.m. each day. At this time, his boss dropped the work assignments into his "in" basket. Shortly thereafter, his stomach began to hurt. In my office, Joe practiced breath abdomen exercises until he felt confident he could apply them in his office. Now, when his boss walks away, Joe takes a few minutes and practices the breath abdomen refresher at his desk. His stomach no longer hurts.

Reaching your Relaxed Core State while Walking

As you walk, do you think of future plans and the past events of your day? Do you stay aware of your breathing as you walk? Do you notice the size of your footsteps? Many people walk and do not pay attention to their thoughts, posture, breathing patterns, or footsteps.

Start reaching your Relaxed Core State while walking by focusing your attention on these four parts. Simply start telling yourself to become aware of your breathing pattern. Tell yourself, "I am now noticing my breathing patterns—breath coming in and breath coming out." Start to pay more attention to your posture and footsteps. You can use this easy process as you are walking anywhere and at any time.

The following exercise demonstrates how to become calmer while you walk:

Breath Walk—In and Out

1. Walk and glance down slightly looking at the tip of your nose.

   • Listen for the sounds of your breath as you inhale and exhale through your nose.
   • Notice whether your breathing sounds slow or fast.
   • Begin to be aware of your posture. Are you standing up straight? Do you have your shoulders back and your head raised?

Or are you finding that your shoulders are hunched?

- Listen to the sound of your footsteps.

  Do you experience them as soft or heavy? Describe the sound of your footsteps.

2. Walk and say to yourself:
   "I am now noticing my breathing patterns.
   BREATH COMING IN as I take one step.
   BREATH COMING OUT as I take the next step."

3. Let yourself have the experience of walking for a few minutes.

   - Keep your attention focused on the inhalation and exhalation of your breath.
   - Notice what happens as you become aware of the sensations in your body.
   - Do you have more awareness of your footsteps?
   - Has your posture improved?
   - How does your breathing sound?
   - Do you feel calmer?

4. Remember to walk in a calm and relaxed fashion. The rhythmic pattern of your footsteps will help you to reach your Relaxed Core State quicker.

5. Practice this exercise for five minutes while walking fast or slow.

   - As you practice concentrating on the sound of your breathing while walking, notice that reaching your Relaxed Core State becomes easier. You can do this exercise anywhere and at any time.
   - If you find yourself feeling stressed at the office, take a five-minute break and practice breath walking as you go to the rest room. Feeling thirsty? Take a few minutes to breath walk before your coffee break. Lunch breaks give you a great opportunity to practice. Practice this breathing technique also when you leave the office. Breath walk anywhere and at any time. This simple exercise has very powerful effects.

Patty, a conference planner, came to me (D.L.) distressed about work thoughts. During every lunch hour, she left the office and went for a walk. She kept thinking about all the work she still had to do when she returned to the office. She simply wanted to use her lunch hour as a refreshing break. She wanted to return to work feeling relaxed and motivated.

Now Patty practices breath walking on the way to lunch and on the way back to the office. She tells me that concentrating on her breath definitely keeps her mind off work thoughts.

I have based the next exercise on the breath abdomen refresher. You will find the steps similar to the breath walking exercise that you have just practiced. As you walk, simply remember to push your abdomen out as you breathe in. To make it easier, as you inhale, imagine that a balloon is filling up with air. Then, pull your abdomen in as you exhale, and, as you do this, picture a balloon deflating. Let's try this exercise and see what changes you feel.

Breath Walk—Abdomen Focus

1. Picture your abdomen as you hear the inhalation and exhalation of breathing sounds from your nose.

2. Now, place either hand on your abdomen. To a count of 5, slowly inhale a long, slow and deep breath as you push your abdomen out. Picture a balloon filling with air.

3. Hold your breath for a count of 5.
   Silently say to yourself:
   1 long inhale
   2 long inhale
   3 long inhale
   4 long inhale
   5 long inhale.

4. After five seconds, slowly exhale through your nose to a count of 5. Pull your abdomen in (see a balloon deflating).

5. Now, focus your attention on your abdomen.
   - Walk and as you inhale, push your abdomen out (see balloon filling up). Say to yourself as you take one step forward to a count of five:
   - **BREATH COMING IN.**
   - As you exhale, pull your abdomen in (see balloon deflating). Say to yourself as you take another step:
   - **BREATH COMING OUT.**

6. Remember to walk in a calm, relaxed fashion. The rhythmic pattern of your footsteps will help you reach your Relaxed Core State more quickly.

7. At first, this exercise may seem a bit difficult. After practicing the steps a few times, it will become second nature to you. Allow yourself to have the experience of walking for a few minutes and keep your attention focused on your abdomen and the inhalation and exhalation of your breath.

8. Notice what happens. Become more fully aware of the sensations in your body.
   - Do you feel more aware of your footsteps?
   - Has your posture improved?
   - How does your breathing sound?
   - Do you feel calmer?

As you focus on your abdomen, concentrate on the sound of your breath while you walk. Notice yourself reaching your Relaxed Core State more easily. Do this exercise for five minutes anywhere and at any time.

If you find yourself feeling nervous at the office, take a five-minute break. During this time, practice the breath abdomen walking as you head to the rest room. Do you find yourself feeling lethargic? Then take a few minutes to breath walk before you reach for that candy bar. Lunch breaks also give you a great time to practice, as does using this breathing technique when you leave the office. You can do abdomen breath walking anywhere and at any time because this really works in a very simple and powerful way.

David came to me (D.L.) because he suffered from a feeling of tightness in his stomach. He especially experienced this feeling when a report or presentation came due. And because he works as a sales manager for a small company, they expect him to give frequent presentations. He told me that the *more* he thinks about giving presentations, the *tighter* his stomach feels. After meeting with me briefly, and practicing the abdomen breath walking, his stomach immediately began to feel better. Today, on his way to work and in his lunch break, he continues to practice the exercise. And he happily tells me that he feels great and his stomach no longer bothers him.

Recapping Day One

- You have now completed the *first day* of the seven-day program. How do you feel? Take a moment now to review your learnings and experiences.

- We started by having you use your *neurological equipment* more fully. If you followed the exercises, you will have discovered how this simple program empowers you to feel more aware of your breath and your posture. Notice how using your heart and lungs to breathe more fully and deeply and using your posture and movements to move gracefully moves you into your Relaxed Core State.

- What else have you learned?

- Stop and notice the thoughts and feelings that come to mind about these breathing and movement exercises.

- Typically, many people learn how disconnected they have been from their bodies—and how they have failed to use these simple tools to manage their state more effectively. Many people say they feel more grounded and centered from just breathing more fully.

- Now that you have learned the lessons of this first day, what will help you to *keep* these learnings and new skills with you? In NLP (Neuro-Linguistic Programming or Processing), the field from which we speak, the process of linking, connecting, or anchoring a learning to something else, gives you a handy tool for retaining these lessons.

- So, for now, think about something which you can use to cue yourself to take a deep breath, to adjust your posture, and to walk in a way which refreshes your energy. You can use a word, an image (internal or external), a symbol, or a sound.

21

- Some examples of visual anchors include:
  - ➥ Seeing pictures of a sun.
  - ➥ Seeing yourself in a relaxed posture.
- Auditory anchors include:
  - ➥ Hearing yourself say, "Relax, slow down."
  - ➥ Hearing the sounds of a waterfall.
- Kinesthetic anchors include:
  - ➥ Letting your hands open.
  - ➥ Touching your heart.

What **anchor** or **reminder** have you chosen or will you choose for yourself to stay in your Relaxed Core State? List them below.

- **Auditory** _____

- **Visual** _____

- **Kinesthetic** _____

Day Two: The Posture of Relaxation

Posture Exercises

Do you sometimes find yourself feeling tired after sitting at your desk for a period of time? If you find yourself slumping in your chair or feel your head tilting forward, these positions will actually contribute to this tired feeling. No wonder then that checking your posture becomes an important part of relaxation skills. Remind yourself that small shifts in your posture can result in helping you to feel more energized and awake.

You can shift your posture by bringing your attention and your awareness to certain parts of your body. It is very important to become aware of your posture, especially while you sit and stand, and to recognize the role it plays in tension and relaxation.

Below we have a checklist indicating common forms of posture while standing and sitting. Notice the difference in posture when you reach your Relaxed Core State and when you remain in a non-relaxed state. As you become aware of how your posture affects you, notice also how it influences your mindset, productivity, and feelings.

Posture Checklist

RELAXED STATE	NON-RELAXED STATE
• Standing up straight	• Standing in slouched position
• Sitting up straight	• Sitting in slouched position
• Centered head	• Head tilted to the right or left
• Loose neck and shoulders	• Tight feeling neck and shoulders
• Shoulders back and down	• Shoulders forward/hunched
• Smiling	• Frowning
• Relaxed facial muscles	• Tight facial muscles
• Relaxed jaw	• Clenched jaw
• Slow, steady breathing	• Fast breathing
• Deep breathing	• Shallow breathing
• Loose hands and fingers	• Hands and fingers forming fists
• Feet relaxed on floor	• Feet tapping the floor
• Open hands	• Clenched hands
• Uncrossed legs	• Crossed legs
• Uncrossed ankles	• Crossed ankles

Reaching your Relaxed Core State using posture exercises

By focusing on certain elements of your body, you can reach your Relaxed Core State quicker. Therefore, it is important to focus on the position of your head, neck, shoulders, and back. The following exercise helps you to feel your Relaxed Core State while sitting.

Relaxed Posture (Sitting) Exercise

1. Find a comfortable position in a chair.

2. Begin slowly to move your elbows back.
   - Do you feel your shoulders moving back?
   - Does your chest expand?
   - Does your breathing become deeper?

3. When you feel ready, slightly tilt your chin up keeping it centered.
   - Do you find that your head tilts back?
   - Does your neck feel looser?
     a. Is your neck in a centered position?
     b. Is your chin in a level position?

4. Now, what happens when you open your palms and point them downward?

- Notice what happens as you imagine that any anxiety and tension that you felt earlier pours out from your hands.

5. Now, pick an object on the wall and look at this object for a couple of seconds.
   - Remember the feeling of relaxation you just felt while you focused your attention on your elbow, shoulders, chin and neck.
   - Continue to look at this object in front of you. Allow yourself to let go and sink deeper into this calm feeling.
   - Imagine this feeling of relaxation growing stronger and surrounding your body, from head to toe.
   - Magnify the peace that you feel. Take a moment and tune into this feeling fully. Step back and take a snapshot of how your body looks. Store this image in your mind and body. This describes how you feel in your relaxed core state—calm, centered, energized, focused, and at ease.
   - Stay in this position for five minutes.
   - And also remind yourself that you created this sensation in just a few minutes, didn't you? Already you have begun to develop the ability to create that final result—**Instant Relaxation.** And we have many more exercises, tools and strategies to enrich your Relaxed Core State.

Reaching your Relaxed Core State using Posture Exercises

Do you have a co-worker who has started to annoy you? Do you have a deadline that you must complete in only half an hour? Do you respond to such events by starting to feel **stressed?**

When you start to feel stressed, take a few minutes, be aware of your posture and make shifts to move yourself into your Relaxed Core State. By investing a few minutes to practice the relaxed focused posture exercise, your life will feel more calm, centered and peaceful. And remember, you now have the ability to reach this state at any time in your office.

Margie works in the marketing department of a large corporation. She came to me (D.L.) complaining that her boss appeared to feel very uncomfortable around her. Each time he called her into his office, she sat in a chair in front of him. She felt that he reacted negatively to her body language, but she did not quite understand why.

Margie had a tendency to twiddle her thumbs and knew that some people found that habit annoying. We discussed the importance of posture while sitting in front of her boss. I explained the importance of keeping her feet parallel and firmly planted on the floor. We also determined that she should keep her hands either in her lap or by her side. These hand positions reminded her *not* to twiddle her thumbs. Now that Margie has become aware of her posture, and especially in front of her boss, he has begun to feel more comfortable. As a result, they have an improved working relationship.

Relaxed Posture (Standing) Exercise

You may find yourself starting to feel tired after you stand for a period of time. If you find yourself slouching over and your head tilting forward, these positions may contribute to this tired feeling. Remember to check your posture and remind yourself that small shifts in your posture will usually result in helping you to feel more energized and awake. This shift in posture happens when you bring your attention and your awareness to certain parts of your body. Focus on the position of your head, neck, shoulders, back, buttocks and feet. The following exercise will help you to feel your Relaxed Core State while standing.

As you answer the following questions, become aware of your normal standing position. This exercise focuses on shifting your posture in order to discover what it feels like to stand in a new way. This new form of posture will also help you to reach your Relaxed Core State.

1. Notice your posture in a standing position.

2. Are your elbows in front of or behind your body?
    a. Do your shoulders slump forward?
    b. Does your chest contract and come forward?

3. Do your feet turn inward or outward?
    a. Do your knees turn inward or outward?

4. Does your chin tilt forward or backward?
    a. Does your head tilt forward or backward?
    b. Does your neck lean forward or backward?

5. Are your palms open or closed?

6. Does your pelvis stick out, causing your back to arch? Does your pelvis tuck in, causing flexion?

The following shifts in posture help you to feel more calm, centered, energized, focused, and at ease. These involve some subtle shifts in movement. The more subtle shifts you make, the quicker you reach your Relaxed Core State.

Shifts in Movement

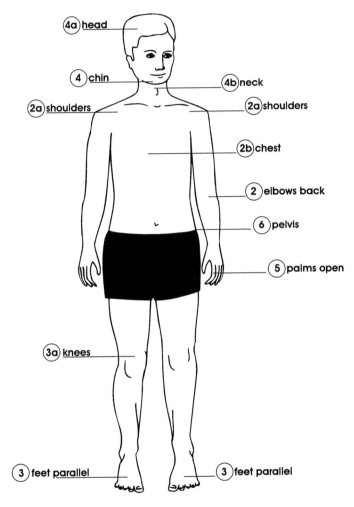

1. Find a comfortable standing position.

2. Now, begin slowly to move your elbows back.
   a. Do you feel your shoulders moving back?
   b. Does your chest expand?
   Does your breathing become deeper?

3. When you feel ready, move your feet so that they are parallel to each other.
   a. After moving your feet parallel, slightly bend your knees and tighten your buttocks.

4. Slightly tilt your chin down.
   a. Does your head straighten out?
   b. Does your neck feel looser?

5. What happens when you open your palms and point them downward?
   Notice what happens as you imagine that all anxiety and tension that you felt earlier now pours out of your hands.

6. Pick an object on the wall.

- Let's say you pick a photo of a turtle.
- Look at this object for a couple of seconds.

Remember the feeling of relaxation you just felt while you focused on your feet, knees, buttocks, elbows, shoulders, chin and neck. Continue to look at this object in front of you. Let this object become your connection, your link, and anchor to your relaxed standing posture. Feel how your body loosens and lets go of holding on to tight muscular patterns in this relaxed standing position.

As you gently do this, allow yourself to expand and sink deeper into this calm feeling. Imagine that this feeling of relaxation magnifies and surrounds your body, from head to toe. Now, allow this soothing, calm feeling to increase. Continue looking at this object and tune into this feeling. Let this object become a reminder of how you feel in your Relaxed Core State. And again, remind yourself that you created this sensation in just a few minutes.

- Stay in this position for five minutes.
- While at the office, you see your boss approaching. Does your abdomen start to churn? If so, take a minute, look at your relaxation object and remember to adjust yourself so you can stand in your relaxation posture. By assuming a relaxed posture, you will have more control over your thoughts and actions.
- By investing a few minutes a day to practice this exercise, the *relaxed standing* posture, your life will feel more calm and peaceful. Remember, you have the ability to reach this state at any time and anywhere. Simply, use the skill of seeing your relaxation object which then relaxes your mind and your body as it brings you into your relaxed core state.

How did you do this? You did it by using the skill of relaxing your body and mind, and by then re-accessing it.

Michelle works as a publicist. She scheduled an appointment with me (D.L.) because her head hurt each time she gave presentations. The thought of standing in front of her colleagues gave her head pains. In our conversation, we reconstructed the room in which she gives her presentations. She chose the clock as her relaxation object and began to practice standing tall and feeling comfortable.

Now when Michelle gives presentations, she finds herself glancing at her favorite clock from time to time. She reminds herself to breathe, relax and therefore to feel herself standing in a confident pose. Her head no longer hurts and her colleagues wonder how she became much more confident overnight.

Recapping Day Two

- This brings us to the end of the first two days. As you have probably noticed, we have focused almost entirely on using your body, your physiology, and various neurological processes to access and solidify your **Relaxed Core State.**

- **Why** does this work?

- **How** does it happen that different movements and using different postures and breathing patterns influences your **state of mind**?

- These exercises work because your mind and body exist and function as a holistic system. This inter-connectedness between mind and body means that you essentially have **royal roads to states.** You can access, develop, amplify, and solidify desired states (such as your Relaxed Core State) by using either your mind or your body.

- **What state of mind** emerges for you when you slump your body, keep your muscles in tight and tense holding patterns, or walk by dragging your feet through the office?

- **What state of mind** emerges when you sit up straight? And when you shake out the tensions in your muscles? When you walk with a feeling of energy inside you, how different do you feel?

- Since mind and body exist and function as an interactive system, this explains **why** the way you use your body plays such a critical and vital role in state management. Later, we will focus on providing you with ways for more effectively using your brain to control your states. We have started with these neurological processes.

- **Why?** Because, generally, most people find it easier to **act** themselves into **new ways of being and experiencing** than thinking their way there.

Day Three: The Eyes of Relaxation

Focused Eye Movements

- Do you find yourself spending hours in front of the computer?
- Do you spend lots of time sending e-mails to office colleagues?
- Do you find yourself reading lots of material for your job?

- If so, then you probably spend many hours with your eyes focused straight ahead in one position, do you not? Yet, when eye muscles stay locked in one position for long periods of time, we generally find that this causes us to become tired. Consequently, we feel eye strain and muscle tension in the head and neck area. Practicing the following series of simple eye movements will give you some ways to relax your eyes.

Four-Object Eye Focus Exercise

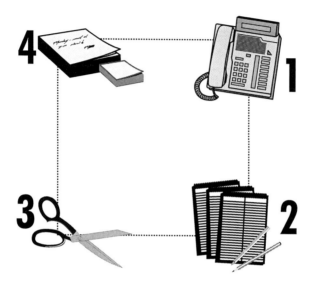

1. Allow yourself to become comfortable while seated at your desk. Find four different points to focus on. Let's say that you select the phone, a message pad, a pair of scissors and Post-its.

2. Focus on the first point, the phone, for ten seconds. As you focus on this phone, hear yourself saying the word **RELAX** in a calm and soothing voice.

3. Now move on to the second object, a message pad. Again, as you focus on this for ten seconds, listen to yourself saying the word **RELAX** in a calm and soothing voice.

4. When you feel ready, move on to the third object, the pair of scissors. Keep looking at the scissors and repeat to yourself the word **RELAX**. After ten seconds, move on to the next point.

5. The last point is the Post-its. Stay focused on this point for ten seconds. Remind yourself to **RELAX** in a calm and soothing voice.

6. Repeat this four-step (steps 2—5) sequence ten more times.

Reaching your Relaxed Core State using eye-focusing movements

During the day, take a few breaks and practice moving your eyes back and forth between four different objects in your office. Choose any four objects that you find around you, for instance, a chair, desk, door knob or wastebasket.

Remember, stay focused on each object for ten seconds. Hear yourself repeating **calming** relaxation messages. The more often you practice this technique, the stronger your Relaxed Core State will become. The next time you feel a tense situation approaching, take a minute and **gently** focus on four relaxation objects of your choice. Now you can let these become reminders that you have the ability to reach your Relaxed Core State at any time and anywhere.

Gary came to me (D.L.) because he could not relax in his office. As a lawyer, he felt the constant pressure of meeting deadlines when writing his briefs. He would feel the pressure mounting with each hour that ticked by. His mind became so focused on the time deadline that he found it difficult to concentrate. His thoughts did not logically follow, and he found himself taking twice as long to complete his assignments.

After meeting with me, he selected four relaxation objects:
- his in-tray
- his law review magazine
- his favorite mug
- his diploma which hung on his office wall

In my office, he closed his eyes, saw himself at work and practiced focusing on these relaxation objects. He practiced for a few minutes and really experienced the feeling of relaxation come over him as he shifted his eyes from one relaxation object to the next. After he became skilled using this eye technique, I had him picture himself at work when he had to meet a deadline. In his chair, he continued to work and also practiced focusing on his relaxation objects. After a few days of practicing and focusing on his relaxation objects, he found himself more productive than ever.

Do you ever find yourself walking into your home and starting to feel stressed because your partner demands that you cook dinner? Then you discover that you have no groceries and yesterday's dishes are still sitting in the sink. Now you have a new eye-focusing skill that you can use to shift into your Relaxed Core State and stay calm and centered.

- Select four objects in your kitchen, for example your dishwasher, toaster, cutting board and stove
- Repeat the four-object eye focus exercise you just practiced
- Remember to repeat this sequence ten times
- **Fully** notice just how much more relaxed you feel and enjoy the power that this state gives you

Diane came to see me (D.L.) because she felt overwhelmed with the demands of career and home. Diane worked as a teacher and would feel absolutely drained after working all day with preschool children. Her feeling of exhaustion did not surprise me. Diane practiced centering herself by focusing on four objects in her kitchen. She quickly found herself feeling much more calm and in control of her state.

Today, she looks forward to returning home and cooking a meal in a relaxed and comfortable environment. She now feels that the process of cooking has become an enjoyable experience because she has taken charge of her own state.

Do you find that "time" often serves as a source of stress for you? Do you find yourself under the pressure of deadlines? Do you find yourself running from one activity to the next? The next time you feel stressed, look at your watch and try this simple exercise:

Reaching your Relaxed Core State using eye-focusing movements

---

Relaxing Eye-Clock Exercise

1. Look at a clock or your watch.

2. Now, follow the hands of the clock or watch. If you do not have hands on your watch or clock, imagine a clock in front of you, or, if you have a digital watch, imagine it transforming into a clock.

3. Hold your eyes on the 12 for ten seconds. At first, you may find this hard. Continue to practice. Soon focusing on the hands of the clock will seem easy. Remind yourself to **Relax.** Hear yourself saying the word **Relaxing** in a smooth, calm voice.

4. When you feel ready, move your eyes to the 3. Continue to focus your eyes on the 3 for ten seconds. Remind yourself to keep **Relaxing.**

5. Now, slide your eyes down to the 6. Keep your eyes focused on the 6 for ten seconds. Remind yourself to **Relax,** in a calm, smooth voice.

6. When you feel ready, shift your eyes up to the 9. Hold for ten more seconds. Remind yourself to keep **Relaxing** more and more.

7. Repeat this sequence ten more times. Each time you repeat the sequence notice how much more relaxed you feel.

Now, when you find yourself pressed for time or having to meet deadlines, what can you do? Simply slow down and take five minutes to look at your watch. Practice shifting your eyes from the 12 round through 3, 6 and 9 back to the 12. As you do, keep telling yourself to **Relax** as you stay focused on each hand position for five seconds. If you do not have a watch with a second hand, draw one on a piece of paper or imagine one. Always reach your Relaxed Core State by following the same sequence of eye movements.

Reaching your Relaxed Core State using eye focusing movements

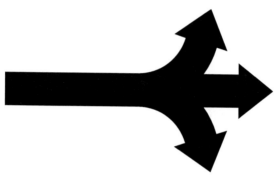

Let us offer yet another exercise for you to play with. This exercise uses the concept of fast and slow time. And it works because you send your brain a message to perform an action using a specific time frame. This action creates a certain result. Let the words **RELAX NOW, SLOW DOWN** become the resource as your eyes focus on the external letters. Let your brain pick up the message and convert the words into a feeling of a relaxed behavior.

Sending the message **SLOW DOWN** in slow motion and in a low tone of voice will convert the feeling behind the words into a similar relaxed behavior. Does this seem magical? The **magic** that we work here involves what we would call **neuro-linguistic magic.** This refers to the mind-body connection that we mentioned earlier and this represents the most basic cognitive behavioral mechanism governing the ways our minds and bodies work as a system. Basically, **as we think—so we feel.**

Reaching your Relaxed Core State using eye-focusing movements

---

Eye-Letter Connection Exercise

So, if you feel nervous at work, find a piece of paper and write the following letters *veerrryy sloooowwly*:

RELAX NOW

SLOW DOWN

Reaching your Relaxed Core State using eye focusing movements
Eye-letter connection exercise

1. After writing each word, hear yourself say these words, **"R E L A X N O W"** very slowly and repeat these words ten times. Each time that you repeat these words, answer the following questions.
   - In this moment, how do you see yourself becoming more relaxed?
   - Can you change your posture or your breathing pattern?
   - How does your voice sound?
   - How do the voices of others sound around you?
   - How relaxing or calming do you find these voices?
   - What kind of quality of voice would sound the most soothing?
   - In this moment, how can you feel even more relaxed?

2. Now, repeat the following words ten times to yourself in **slow motion:**

SLOW DOWN
(S SS SS SS L L L L O O W W W W
DDDD DD OOOO WWWW NNNNN)

- After repeating these words ten times, how do you see your-self **S L O W I N G   D O W N**? Can you change your posture or your breathing pattern?
- How does your voice sound?
- Can you slow down the sound of your voice?
- How do the voices of others around you sound?
- Can you also slow down their voices?
- Do you feel yourself slowing down?

Stacy came to me (D.L.) feeling overwhelmed by her latest promotion. Since she worked as a systems analyst, her job required her to work with computers. She had begun to spend more hours each day at the office. As she did, her boss increased her workload and gave her many more assignments.

Yet she felt she could complete only so many tasks in a day. And the idea of time passing by so quickly made her feel nervous. She always felt that she was behind in her assignments and was not completing enough work.

She would remind herself of the daily deadlines she faced and found herself feeling even more tense when she arrived home in the evening. But when she began practicing the eye-letter connection exercise and seeing the words

> # Relax Now, Slow Down

she felt calmer and more in control of her life. Now, she has a new tool. Whenever she starts to feel those old anxious feelings during the day, she simply stops, writes these words down a few times and reclaims her own sense of self and time.

Recapping Day Three

Going deeper to understand why these processes work

In this last exercise we introduced some age-old concepts. Previously held beliefs said that a person would have to learn the meditative arts for years, even decades, before they could access such powerful resources.

Today, however, you no longer have to go through such long and arduous training. Knowing that every **experience** has a **structure,** an internal form and process, you can avoid all of the content stuff and go straight to the structure. NLP calls this **modeling.** This means that you shift focus from the content to the structure.

The last chapter gave you the techniques, tools, and strategies which provide you with the resources to reach your Relaxed Core State. In the past, the content consisted of longer exercises and practice for much longer periods of time.

Regarding **fast** and **slow time** —we have all had, and continue to have, such experiences. Think of an occasion when "time" went really fast. You were involved in an activity—and suddenly, when you looked up, two hours had passed, but it seemed like only a few minutes. Since external objective **time** did not change, your brain and nervous system alone created this experience. And that means that, if you find the structure of how you did that, you can do it again whenever you choose.

Think about an occasion when "time" nearly stood still, when it went by really, really slowly. Where were you? And under what circumstances? Have you ever driven for a long time on the Interstate at seventy-five mph, then suddenly you turned off and began creeping along at thirty mph? Didn't it seem like "time" itself had slowed down? Again, your brain has created this experience for you.

Just like getting in touch with your **Relaxed Core State** which you are learning to build and then utilize whenever and wherever you wish, you can also achieve a greater awareness of control over your sense of psychological time. Fascinated by this? See Bodenhamer & Hall, (1997) *Time-Lining: Patterns For Adventuring In Time.*

Another point to consider is that Stacy attempted, as do so many of us, to stop worrying about things by telling herself "not to worry." This highlights the power of human **neuro-linguistics.** After all, the word **not** only exists as a negation in linguistics. This means that the word does not exist outside a human brain. To try not to think of blue, of Bill Clinton, of Niagara Falls, of black ice cream, of orange monkeys, necessitates that you first represent such and then try to make the idea go away.

In other words, telling yourself what **not** to do ("I won't worry about that") tends to magnetize the worry so that it becomes more glued to the mind. Certainly you will have noticed this.

So what can you do about it? You can state what **you do want**—comfort, relaxation, peace, ease, health, wholeness, congruency, strength, etc. You can **positively state** what to do, rather than what **not** to do or what you want rather than what you do not want. Doing so will then cue your brain to know what to represent and tell your body what to feel.

Day Four: The Ears of Relaxation

Affirmations—The Ideas and Linguistics of Relaxation

Do you believe in the power of positive thinking? Countless books have been written on this subject. Recent scientific studies have indicated that positive thinking lowers stress and increases health in the body. Do you think of yourself as a positive person who still finds negative thoughts filling your mind? Or, have you perhaps developed a conditioned habit to expect the worst? Whatever your answer, you can train yourself to expect the best, if you want to.

In this fourth day of learning **Instant Relaxation Exercises,** you will practice using affirmations to keep yourself feeling calm, relaxed, and positive. When you feel at ease, you will notice that your breathing also seems deeper and smoother. The following affirmations remind you to stay *positive* as you sit and stand, breathe, walk, and focus on the world around you. This means you will look for value and learn how to put a positive frame on things.

During your day, select and practice one of the three affirmations from each category. After you repeat each affirmation, notice if any changes happen in your body.

- Does your breathing change?
- Do you breathe faster or more slowly?
- Does your posture shift?
- How do you feel?

First, you will want to find an affirmation that feels right. Then when you see a stressful situation coming your way or hear voices that trigger a feeling of tension, start repeating the affirmation to yourself. The more times you practice these affirmations, the faster you will reach your Relaxed Core State.

Reaching Your Relaxed Core State with Affirmations

Breath affirmations
- Deep Hourly Breath
- Quick Breath
- The Relaxing Breath

The deep hourly breath and affirmation
- "I am aware of my breathing throughout the day"
- "At the beginning of each hour, I take ten deep breaths, slowly inhaling and slowly exhaling through my nose"
- "I see, hear and feel myself becoming more and more relaxed with each breath that I take"

The quick breath and affirmation
- "I start off the beginning and end of each hour with ten quick breaths"
- "I quickly inhale and exhale through my nose. This rapid sequence of breathing brings me additional energy"

The relaxing breath and affirmation
- "As I breathe deeply, I relax more fully"
- "My breath helps me to relax"
- "As I inhale, I become more relaxed"
- "As I exhale, I become even more relaxed"

Breath walking affirmations
"Nose Breathing," "Abdomen Breathing"
- "When I walk, I remember to breathe in through my nose. I become aware of my breathing patterns as I listen to the sounds of my breath"
- "At the end of each half-hour, I walk and practice abdomen breathing. I feel my abdomen moving in and out as I breathe"

Posture affirmations
- Posture Sitting Check
- Posture Standing Check

Posture Sitting Check
- "I give myself permission to use the power of relaxation to make me feel more calm and focused"
- "I am aware of my posture throughout the day"
- "At the beginning of each hour, I check that my posture is comfortable"
- "I check to make sure that I am sitting in a relaxed position I feel if I have my back in a straight position, if I have pulled back my shoulders, if I have my chin located in the middle, and if my neck feels relaxed"

Posture Standing Check
- "I joyfully notice my posture throughout the day in order to build my Relaxed Core State"
- "At the beginning of each hour, I check that I stand in a comfortable position"
- "I make sure to keep my feet parallel, my knees slightly bent, and my buttocks slightly tightened. I pull my shoulders back and keep my head straight"

Focusing
- Eye-focus Affirmation—Four-object focus
- Eye-clock Affirmation
- Eye-letter Connection Affirmation

Eye-Focus Affirmation—Four-object focus
- "When I find myself starting to feel stressed, I practice the four-object focus exercise. As I look at four different objects for ten seconds, I remind myself to relax. I repeat this eye sequence ten times"

Eye-Clock Affirmation
- "When I find myself pressed for time, I take a moment to look at my watch. I practice the relaxed eye-clock exercise. I look at my watch and focus on the 12, 3, 6, 9 and 12, reminding myself to relax at each time interval. I repeat this sequence ten times"

Eye-Letter Connection Affirmation

- "When I feel stressed, I write on a sheet of paper:

RELAX NOW

SLOW DOWN

I look at these words for ten seconds and feel the effect of this language as it calms, centers and focuses my body. I write these words down ten times"

Commitment to the core state and affirmation

- Commitment to Positive Thoughts

Commitment to Relaxed Core State

- "I make a commitment to mastering the Relaxed Core State. I achieve this state when I become calm, centered, focused, energized and at ease. No obstacle or challenge will interfere with my state of relaxation"

Commitment to Positive Thoughts

- "I now make a promise to myself—a promise to reward myself with a life full of ease, peace, calmness and a relaxed state of being. If I think negative thoughts, I immediately become aware of how I am affected. I will think of thoughts that I find positive and uplifting"

All of these affirmations which relate to breath, posture, and focusing techniques describe **frames of reference** which you can use as **internal resources** to keep you in your Relaxed Core State. This means that completing the action of the affirmation puts you in touch with your Relaxed Core State.

The actions that you take, such as breathing with awareness **(BREATH REFRESHER exercise),** creates a state of calm and focused attention. This state falls into the Relaxed Core State. Expanding this idea further, you can see that all relaxation behaviors—breathing, shifting your posture, and practicing focusing techniques—create more resourceful states inside yourself.

These states, as frames of reference, tell you how your behavior causes you to feel inside. When you feel out of touch with your Relaxed Core State, simply remember to repeat the affirmation and do the behavior suggested in the affirmation.

Larry, a massage therapist, came to see me (D.L.) because he felt his body getting tense. He had a very successful practice and could not understand why he often felt tired. After asking him a series of questions, I determined that his breathing seemed shallow and that he had poor posture.

Through the interview, I discovered that Larry frequently hunched his shoulders while he gave massages. This body position caused his muscles to tighten, and he further increased the tension by standing in this position for long periods of time. We worked on his becoming more aware of his posture. We figured out a way for him to stand straighter while massaging his clients. He also became aware of his breathing and practiced several breath exercises. Now Larry repeats the breathing and posture affirmations while he gives his massages.

Why Affirmations Work

The power of language lies in its ability to induce states and to create higher level resources. The form of these states include conceptual, abstract, and concrete states that have a neurological form. Therefore, we can learn and master the art of cueing our mind and bodies for healthful states of rest, tranquillity, peace, integration, wholeness, energy, centeredness, etc. These states tremendously affect our overall well-being.

Regarding the process of languaging, lots of people simply do **not** know how to talk to themselves (or others) in kind and gentle ways. Their internal critics rage away—insulting, blaming, accusing, and labeling.

The first step in **really** getting a good handle on this involves **becoming more conscious about your self-talk.** To find out **what** you actually do and say to yourself, you have to tune into that self-talk. You may also have to **turn it up a bit** in order to hear it clearly.

Consider the effect of a very, very, slow, and barely audible voice continually criticizing yourself in an angry tone. Would it not operate almost like a post-hypnotic suggestion? And the fact that it occurs at a barely audible volume only reinforces it as it makes it more difficult to catch and stop those voices. **But you can.** You only have to listen and challenge these voices.

How? Begin by appointing a friend who you trust will have your best interests at heart. Have your friend monitor your self-talk and help you to notice what you're saying. Find a sheet of paper and journal those **automatic thoughts** which go racing through your mind.

Once **you become aware** of the stress and pressure self-talk language causes, go ahead and challenge it.

- Challenge it for accuracy, reality test it and check it for ecology.
- Does it serve you well?
- Would you want anybody else talking to you that way?
- Would you keep a friend who said those things to you?

Next, invent and create all types of words, phrases, and lines to use on yourself that will work much better. You can use words which meet the **criteria** of kind, gentle, true, empowering, etc. The **affirmation language** given here provides just an introduction as to how to use language to channel and govern consciousness. Start discovering and paying attention to the sensory-based world around you. You can also use affirmations to affirm and assert new ways of coping and mastering things. Use affirmations to discover new ways of being in the world and to find for yourself more resourceful ways to think and respond.

Ultimately, your particular brand of consciousness consists of a **languaged consciousness.** This means that you form and mold your consciousness according to how you have been languaged and how you continue to language yourself. Ready for some more languaging?

Recapping Day Four

Want to know more?

When you make a commitment to your **Relaxed Core State,** you set a **frame** in your life. This **frame** then becomes **a higher level resource.** And as your **frame of reference,** it orients you about what to do in life, the choices you make and how you decide to live your life, etc. A commitment like that becomes a **value** that you believe in.

Your values also exist as a **state of mind-and-body about another state**—the primary state of relaxation. As a state-about-a-state, it can exist then as a calmness, centeredness, etc. You have actually created more than just one resource, you have created two. At the primary level, you have focused on becoming relaxed and whole. And at a Meta-level, you have **committed** yourself to that. You have made an empowering decision about it.

What does this mean?

Establishing a **Meta-state of commitment for your Relaxed Core State** enables you to not have to **think** about relaxing all the time. Like any other *frame* of reference, once it gets established and set, it will simply run the show. **It will become part of your very perceptions about how you look at the world. This *state* (commitment) about another state (the primary state of your *Relaxation Core State*)** protects and solidifies that state.

Day Five: The Internal Imagery of Relaxation

Visualizations

Reaching your Relaxed Core State with Mind Affirmations and Mind Visualizations

Do you think of yourself as a positive person who sometimes thinks negative thoughts and then wonders, "Why does this happen to me?" Many possible causes could explain this state of thinking.

Your conditioning and experience with various past events inevitably play the central role in the way your mind works. You can analyze and try to determine the cause. You can also take action and start reading, seeing, and repeating positive affirmations to yourself. These visualization-affirmations relax your mind and help you to reach your Relaxed Core State quickly and effortlessly.

In the following affirmations, allow your mind to visualize scenes, events, objects, and symbols, whether real or imagined, that will assist you in the process of accessing your Relaxed Core State. Find the affirmations which most shift you into your Relaxed Core State.

Mind visualization-affirmations
- Accepting my mind
- Changing my mind
- Empowering my mind
- Energizing my mind
- Enjoying my mind
- Opening my mind
- Protecting my mind
- Resting my mind
- Strengthening my mind
- Thanking my mind
- Understanding my mind

Instant Relaxation Exercises

Reaching your Relaxed Core State with Mind Visualization-affirmations, Beliefs, Values and Understandings

Accepting my mind
- "I will become open-minded, accepting, and non-judgmental toward others"

Changing my mind
- "My life sometimes feels like a roller coaster with lots of ups and downs"
- "My ups make me feel amazing and ecstatic"
- "I also know that I will face various downs which lie ahead of me"
- "I will remain open to the unpredictable curves in my life and simply prepare myself for the next uphill ride"
- "I know all of these experiences simply function as a part of living life"

Empowering my mind
- "Today I empower myself to do what I love to do"
- "I find books, magazines and movies that inspire me and make me feel creative"
- "I bring meaning to my life through helping, contributing and just being me"

Energizing my mind
- "I energize my mind as I give myself permission to practice breath exercises"
- "The more I breathe, the more oxygen flows into my brain enabling me to think more clearly"

Enjoying my mind
- "My life feels as if I walk on an infinite trail. I always enjoy the journey"
- "I remain patient and aware with each step that I take"
- "I remain open to possibility and change"
- "I remain flexible in my thinking as I walk along the path of life"

Reaching your Relaxed Core State with Mind Visualization-affirmations

Opening my mind
- "Everyday I open my mind to new thoughts, ideas, possibilities, perspectives, and beliefs"
- "I view myself as a special person with my own unique set of views and philosophies about life"
- "I do not waste my energy on toxic people and situations"
- "I have the right to choose my own voice and thoughts"

Protecting my mind
- "I take care to protect myself from people and situations that drain me of energy"
- "I surround myself with happy and encouraging people"
- "I do not need to waste energy on toxic people and situations. I can simply walk away from them, and continue with my life"

Resting my mind
- "Even if I feel quiet, reserved and introverted, I listen to and observe others around me"
- "During that time, I fill myself with energy and internal strength"
- "I feel confident and secure with myself"
- "I know that I can share myself and my ideas when I feel ready"

Reaching your Relaxed Core State with Mind Visualization-affirmations

Strengthening my mind
- "I strengthen my mind by practicing Instant Relaxation Exercises"
- "I learn to focus my mind and achieve the goals I set for myself"

Thanking my mind—Changing My Attitude
- "Today I have a positive attitude"
- "I feel grateful for the things I have"
- "I know many people around the world have much less than I"
- "I stop comparing myself to others"
- "I know my life will stay on the track that I have set"
- "I go further by smiling, being happy and encouraging others"

Understanding my mind
- "I understand that my mind makes decisions that best suit me"
- "I make my thoughts and decision-making processes align themselves with my goals in life"

Becky, a social worker, came to me (D.L.) complaining that she felt sick and tired of her profession. At the beginning of her career, she enjoyed listening to the problems of others. But now, she had arrived at a point where she felt worn and drained from constantly listening to people repeating the same stories time and time again. She told me that her clients just kept repeating the same mistakes over and over again. Becky selected the visualization-affirmation, "thanking my mind." She found repeating this visualization-affirmation very powerful.

Now, before and after meeting with clients, she practices this visualization-affirmation. She tells me that she feels much happier and looks at her clients in a more understanding way.

Feelings of stress and relaxation both start in the mind. Depending on **how** you **interpret** your behavior or the behavior of others, *you create* stressful or relaxed feelings inside of you. This cognitive behavioral mechanism explains both the simplicity, yet profundity, of change. Of course, we have many other choices in terms of our reactions to another's behavior. Studies have shown that we can tremendously influence our states of behavior by our beliefs and values.

For example, if Becky, the social worker, believes that listening to the problems of people all day long feels tiring, then typically that will result in her body becoming tired. If she highly values helping people, and yet she feels tired, she could shift her value of not giving it so much importance.

If she doesn't, she will grow tired of listening to other people's problems. Or perhaps she could slip into a very ineffective

listening style. She could listen and represent **associated-ly** so that she uses the information of problems that she hears to put herself into feeling states. Such **"sympathy"** representation would enable her to "feel what the other feels," yet at the same time it may reduce her effectiveness as a people helper.

On the other hand, if she redefines her mission in life in terms of becoming empathic, caring, and unconditionally loving, then the behavior of listening and talking all day long would refresh and invigorate her. In this case, she **empathizes** (rather than sympathizes). The difference? She can now "enter into the person's world" without having to experience the other's emotions. She can **"see and hear"** the world as the client does, and yet stay **out of it.** This makes more sense in terms of operating as a people helper.

The point in all of this—learning to see how our beliefs and values strongly influence our behavior. By repeating the mind visualizations, our beliefs and values come in line with those of a person experiencing and living from a **RELAXED CORE STATE.**

In fact, this might make for a good way to test your thinking. **Does it facilitate a more Relaxed Core State?** If it does not, the thinking will probably not serve you well.

You see how your beliefs and values strongly influence your behavior. By repeating the mind visualizations, your beliefs and values become in line with those of a person who experiences living from a **RELAXED CORE STATE.**

Visualization-relaxation Thoughts

Beliefs/Frames/Meta-states

Now that you have attuned your ears and have begun to listen closely to your language, do you hear thoughts that block you from achieving your full potential? Have you ever thought, "If only I had a system, or a way of thinking, that could help me move from feeling stuck to unstuck? If only I could let go of thoughts that hold me down and replace these thoughts with uplifting, empowering thoughts?"

With Day Five, we now add new dimensions to the affirmations. Here we will move beyond just **mere** thoughts—representations of enhancing pictures, sounds, and sensations for your internal movie screen. We want to use the **affirmations** of various beliefs to solidify and strengthen these thoughts.

A belief differs from a thought. When you think a thought, you have represented various visual, auditory, and kinesthetic information. You may have also represented information in the form of languaged ideas (words). Yet, you can *think* many thoughts that you do not *believe.* You can entertain ideas from others and even understand them with clarity and force, and still not *believe in* them.

When you do *believe* in a thought, you experience *a confirmation about the thought.* This means that, at a Meta-level, you make an affirmation about the thought. For example, take the fact that you can think lots of thoughts which you do not believe. Think of something that you definitely do not believe. Can you do it? Of course. You can think about any idea and say "No, no way!" to that idea.

Now think of something that you do believe. Here, you thought a *thought,* and you believed or affirmed that thought. You say, "Yes, of course!" to that idea. With beliefs, often the thoughts which make up the belief are unconscious and not in your awareness.

Now, you can use the following relaxation thoughts to help you in seeing new patterns to adhere to in your life and which will provide you with a fresh way of viewing your world. Read through the following relaxation thoughts with a sense of **affirmation** and **confirmation** of **"Yes!"** about those thoughts.

See and feel the situations you can apply to your life on your internal mental screen. When you feel ready to shift your thinking, begin to apply the action steps which will help you to reach your Relaxed Core State.

Visualization-relaxation thoughts

"My past does not equal my future"
"My persistence will pay off"
"I will improve every day"
"I will make my vision a reality"
"My life is always full of surprises"
"I will just 'Go For It!'"
"I will make a decision today"

Visualization-relaxation thoughts

How easy do you find it to imagine yourself feeling great and empowered most of the time? If you don't, do you find it stressful to not feel in control of your mind? Feeling resourceful most of the time becomes a possibility when you know *how to run your own brain*. I have designed the following relaxation thoughts to assist you in moving forward when you feel stuck. Read through the topics and visualize yourself participating in these activities. Feel wonderful as you do, and then take action.

My past does not equal my future

Just for a minute, think of a successful person who came from behind and beat the odds. If you do not know a person of this type, think about someone you have seen on television or heard on the news.

Once you have selected someone, see how this person sits or stands and look at their posture. Hear this person speaking and feel their enthusiasm for life. You could choose someone living, or a great leader from the past like Martin Luther King, Gandhi, Lincoln, Churchill, etc.

How do you imagine this person continues to keep an enthusiastic and upbeat attitude regardless of all situations and endeavors that did not work out? Do you think this person has a strategy for overcoming disappointments? What phrases does this person tell him or herself? How does this person move on? How does this person adapt to new situations?

Often in life, you face disappointments. When this happens, you can choose to learn from your past trials and failures and continue to step forward with a new set of beliefs. Or you can choose to become upset and hold on to your feelings of sadness or anger.

You can look at all past events as a learning experience. Let's say your boss fires you. How can you turn this situation into a positive experience? Maybe you can look for a better job. You can re-evaluate your current situation and decide what you liked and disliked about this job. You can evaluate your strengths and weaknesses.

This process may give you a better understanding of your skills and allow you to make educated decisions about future jobs. Reflect on the benefits of starting a new job. Perhaps, you may meet nicer people and have greater opportunities for advancement.

In the present, unexpected jolts such as relationship upsets or career changes may appear jarring. But, as you step into the future, **gently let go** of your past. Take a step forward and think of your future as a new chapter in your life. Think about your goals and your objectives in life. Know that you live in a country of opportunity and abundance. Recognize yourself as the creator of your world.

Observe the language that you use to describe your actions. Use words that create action. Use such phrases as:

"I'm looking for a job that makes me feel like I'm contributing."
"I'm working on starting a new job where my talents can be best utilized."
"I'm looking for a job in the recording studio or any other desired location."
- Remember to stay focused on your goals and objectives
- Your actions and the tasks that you accomplish today determine your future. Each morning, you can consider your past as finished. You now have a choice about shaping the future you desire.

My persistence will pay off

When you want to do something and it does not work out, do you give up easily? Or do you take a step back and ask yourself what you can learn? Do you believe that, if one strategy does not work, you can simply shift to another strategy?

Endless ways exist to accomplish tasks and reach your goals. Approach problem-solving tasks from differing perspectives. Let's use the scenario that you want a perfect job in advertising as an example. You want a job in the media planning department of an advertising company. You send out fifty letters to the media planning department. After one month, you get back ten negative responses.

Now, do you find yourself feeling very upset and find it difficult to move forward? Do you start telling yourself that you will never succeed and that no one will hire you? Or do you think of another strategy? Maybe, you decide to volunteer as an intern in the media planning department. Or maybe you decide to find successful people in advertising and arrange interviews. Remember, the key to success lies in **staying focused** on your goals. Keep testing new strategies which help to accomplish your goals.

Another effective strategy to accomplishing your goals involves **modeling.** Modeling means looking at successful people and then learning from their strategies. Read books on the most successful people in your field. Find out how they succeeded. Isolate their skills and work on building these skills into yourself. Ask them about the qualities they found necessary to succeed. Ask them for tips on succeeding. Each day, remember to take small action steps. Make yourself a promise and try a new technique each day. We want to use the affirmations of various beliefs.

We have already noted that a belief differs from a mere thought. When we move from a thought to a belief, we move to a Meta-level and *affirm* or *confirm* the thought. Believing involves saying a big, bold **Yes!** to the ideas that we want to turn into "beliefs."

Use the following relaxation thoughts to help you in seeing new patterns to follow in your life and which will provide you with a fresh way of viewing your world. Read through the following relaxation thoughts with a sense of **affirmation** and **confirmation** of "Yes!" about those thoughts.

See and feel the situations you can apply to your life on your internal mental screen. When you feel ready to shift your thinking, begin to apply the action steps which will help you to reach your Relaxed Core State.

I will improve every day

Do you find interesting people around you? Do you see people whom you have wanted to meet for some time? Do you have some books that you keep looking at on your bookshelf? Do you know of some classes that you want to take? If so, prioritize these tasks into your life. You can learn so much from a single conversation or by reading a chapter of a book, if you have an open and relaxed mind.

You can also learn a lot by watching an informative television show. Each day, challenge yourself and do something different. Talk to a stranger, read a book, a magazine, or watch an educational show. Open your eyes and open your ears to the sounds of learning which always surround you. Continue to ask yourself each day, **"How can I become more effective in the various areas of my life?"**

I will make my vision a reality

Have you ever seen a picture that captures an ideal scene of beauty? Can you imagine a long white sandy beach with palm trees and turquoise water? This represents just one concept of a beautiful scene. Everyone has their own interpretation of beauty. Now, paint a picture in your mind of a goal you have. See this goal turn into a vision. This goal may represent your highly desired job, perfect relationship, or vacation.

Let's use my ideal job as an example. When I imagine my perfect job, I see a beautiful office. The walls are covered with nature photographs. I see furniture made of mahogany and a large floral display on the window sill. Now, I would like you to see, hear, and feel many more details of your highly desired job. What type of voices do you hear? What types of sounds do you hear in your office?

When you feel ready, cut pictures out. Construct a collage that brings together all the elements of your perfect job. Include pictures, for instance, of mahogany desks, photographs of nature, different floral arrangements, different types of carpeting. Keep adding pictures to your collage that reflect your ideal office and job. While you construct your collage, hear yourself talking to your colleagues. Imagine what you are talking about. Allow yourself to begin to feel the excitement and passion that comes with having your ideal job. Notice what emotions you feel. Do you feel happy and ecstatic?

When you finish your collage, make a few copies of it. Place it on your refrigerator, bathroom and night table. Each time that you look at your collage, remember how good it will feel once you find your ideal job and let those feelings pull you into that future. Let them govern your everyday activities that will contribute to making it real.

Reaching your Relaxed Core State with Visualization-relaxation thoughts

My life is always full of surprises

Have you ever had unpredictable surprises thrown your way? When that happens, how do you react? Do you react with passion? Or do you stand back and let the opportunity pass?

Think about your life and a goal that you have. For example, let's use receiving a promotion at work as your goal. We have different ways for obtaining this goal. You could go into work every day and assume that after one year you will get a promotion. Another approach would involve **developing a plan** for how to get a promotion. You could tell your boss that you want to do the very best job possible. Ask her to correct you immediately when you make a mistake. Have you created a system for correcting mistakes? Show your boss that you can learn quickly and that you can handle more responsibility. Keep a list of your job tasks on your desk and keep adding to this list.

Other steps to take include copying or modeling the most successful people in your desired job. Ask yourself why they have become successful. Start looking at their organizational style and system. How do they organize their desk? Start listening to the words they use as they talk to you and others. What communication styles do they use? Do they command or suggest in their requests? What qualities characterize their personality? Do you experience this person as friendly, calm, or aloof?

Modeling and observing successful people provides us with multiple clues to their success. Doing this does not mean that you copy all aspects of the person. Simply become aware of what they do successfully. Once you have done this, you can begin to incorporate some of these changes that you like into your work style.

Your promotion may not come quickly. But keep working hard and remaining observant. Each day aim to carry out your job tasks in a quicker and more effective way. Continue to speak as if you held a higher position. Doing these things will give you more confidence for feeling that your promotion waits just around the corner. Soon your boss will call you in and tell you the good news.

Reaching your Relaxed Core State with Visualization-relaxation thoughts

I will just "Go for it"

Do you find yourself clinging on to your last failure? Do you feel rejected, depressed, or defeated because of your failure? Do you feel it is difficult to let go of these feelings in order to move forward? If you see yourself tightly holding on, then take a breath and make the decision that you will feel good.

Let's use a misunderstanding at work as an example. Let's say that you ask your colleague to finish some work that you cannot get done. She says, "Sorry, I'm so overwhelmed and I do not have time." But your boss needs you to finish the assignment tonight. You know that your colleague has time, but will not say yes. You may consider the behavior of your colleague to be a big problem. Instead of looking at this as a problem, however, start to view this a challenge.

As you do so, begin by asking yourself, "What kind of solution can I create to overcome this challenge?" Start thinking also about different ways to ask your colleague for help. You may want to ask her again, nicely, telling her how *urgent* your boss considers this project. Or you may want to explain that your boss will become very upset if the work is not completed.

You could even mention that you will tell the boss about your colleague's unhelpfulness. If your colleague does not budge, you may want to raise your voice and tell your colleague that your boss will get really upset by her attitude. Tell her that the consequences will get serious if she does not help you. This approach may work for you. *How you interpret and react* to the situation determines your success.

"Today I take steps to change my life. I know that everyone has problems, disappointments, and frustrations. I do not attach myself to mine. Nor do I waste time getting upset about them. I see, hear, feel, accept, and let my disappointments go. *How* I choose to deal with my setbacks shapes my life. Today I decide to just go for it."

Reaching your Relaxed Core State with relaxation thoughts

I will make a decision today

Have you ever thought about *the power* of your decisions? Do you realize how much your decisions influence your life?

Let's say you make a decision to look for a new job. This decision can change your life. Will you look for a job that provides more opportunity? Will you look for a job that provides different tasks than you currently do? Or will you look for a job in a completely different field? Whatever decision you make heavily influences the course of your life.

If you decide to look for a job with more responsibility, then you need to sharpen your skills and/or possibly learn new skills. Find out the new job tasks and then start assessing your current knowledge. Ask yourself questions that analyze your strengths and weaknesses. Imagine and hear yourself speaking to work colleagues from a position of authority.

Then take the next step. Namely, acknowledge that you cannot always control the events in your life. The type of job you are looking for may be scarce. Or perhaps a company you had hoped to work for just filled this position. You cannot control those things. What can you control? **Mainly your thoughts and beliefs.** You can tell yourself that you will become the best candidate for the job. Then, the next time a job opportunity appears, you have already done much of the preparation and most probably will be the most successful person at the interview. This increases your chances of being hired. In the meantime, you can practice interview techniques and refining your speaking skills.

If you have an interview and it does not go well, do you get upset or can you remain objective? You completely control the interpretation of events that happen to you. Several reasons come to mind as to why you may not have been hired. Perhaps the employer needs aggressive employees, and that does not fit with your style. Remember, your interpretation of situations determines and shapes your future.

When Michelle first came to me (D.L.) she felt very sad and depressed. After working with a company for ten years as an art director, they laid her off. The company had lost a major account and could no longer afford her. I discussed the idea of visualizing a future career and imagining the type of lifestyle she now wanted to have. We discussed the visualization-relaxation thoughts.

My life is full of surprises and **I make my vision a reality.**

In response, she created a collage for her ideal job and the type of accounts she hoped to be put in charge of. When she left my office, she had already begun feeling upbeat, enthusiastic, and in control of her destiny.

Recapping Day Five

Visualization-relaxation thoughts

Now, you have practiced listening to your thoughts and have started developing awareness of the beliefs which hold you back. You now have some visualization-relaxation thoughts that you can use to empower yourself and help yourself move forward when you feel stuck in your thoughts and behavior.

You also have some powerful relaxation thoughts with which you can replace the old, disempowering thoughts. You have the tools to see the patterns in your life and the way you look at the world: **your perceptual filters.** And you have discovered the importance of a positive attitude to enhancing pictures, sounds, and sensations for your internal movie screen.

All of these thoughts continually move you closer to your goals and outcomes. You can continue to experience your Relaxed Core State as you go through this process.

Day Six: The Triggers of Relaxation

Pattern Interrupts

Sometimes, before you can feel calm, centered, focused, energetic and at ease, you have to stop the flow of the thoughts that are currently racing through your head. **Pattern Interrupts** describe one process that we can use for doing precisely this. Thus, we can interrupt states of thoughts and emotions that keep us tense, distracted, preoccupied, and in a state of **dis-ease.**

Imagine the following situation: you have arrived at work and find your boss very upset. She says she expected the assignment she gave you yesterday to have now been completed, and on her desk this morning. Yet, she forgot to tell you about that deadline. Oops! And further, you also forgot to ask about the time she wanted it completed. She yells at you in front of colleagues. As a result, you also feel very upset. What do you do?

You have a choice. You can interrupt your hurt feelings and the spiraling negative state. Or you can remind yourself to stay relaxed and calm by focusing on your **Posture, Breath, Thoughts, Feelings** and **Language.** Of course, to do either of these things you will probably have to first interrupt the unproductive anchors in the process. **And how in the world do you do that? Notice that, in the following sections, we have identified various facets of your mind-body system that you can use to interrupt that state.**

Posture

- If you find yourself slouching, pull your shoulders back and straighten your spine.
- If you find your hands and fists clenched, simply open your hands.
- If you walk quickly, then slow down and breathe.

Breath

- When a stressful situation like this happens, focus on your breath for a few minutes.
- If you find your breathing becoming fast due to angry feelings, take a few deep slow breaths and, as you do, just notice how you begin to slow yourself down by simply doing this.

Thoughts

- Decide *how* you want to interpret the situation. When your boss goes back into her office, play the scene back again.
- Now let yourself see yourself standing across the office and imagine your boss talking to you.
- Hear your boss speaking in a soft voice. Watch the resourceful you smile at your boss. Think about the next step you can take to make things work out more effectively. Let yourself imagine a way to approach your boss and to rectify the situation. What action steps can you take to improve the situation?

Feelings

- Do you feel hurt by the language used by others? Remember that, when your boss reacts, he or she does so without thinking. It reflects their poor state. And you can feel fortunate that *you don't have to* yell at someone to make your point or be effective. Feel grateful that you have a much better style, and will develop an even better style as you continue to learn and practice the Instant Relaxation Exercises.

Language

- Hear the voice of your boss sounding more pleasant.
- Hear your boss speaking softly and slowly. You can also imagine that a good friend stands in place of your boss.
- Notice what happens to your voice as you see these images and hear your boss sounding different. How do you feel?

Al, a salesman, works for a medium size telecommunications firm. He had several problems with his sales manager and he came to see me (D.L.). He did not like the sound of his manager's voice and had a hard time listening to him because of that voice. Then his manager became upset because he felt that Al made mistakes due to his not listening.

Al now applies a few of the pattern interrupt techniques when his manager works with him. He can now hear his boss talking to him in a calm and cool voice. Al's manager also feels very pleased with his ability to listen. Due to his new skills, Al's sales figures have begun to rise.

Relaxation Anchors

Relaxation anchors refer to our resources and signals that stimulate us and remind us to feel calm, centered, focused, energetic, at ease. We can create these anchors by using different parts of our body. We can use a wide range of words, sounds, sights, thoughts and feelings as anchors.

As an example of an *anchor*, think about when you hear an old song. Does it bring back a delightful memory? It works like a trigger in that it evokes from within you thoughts and feelings and thereby puts you into a pleasant state. Here, we will look at anchors which involve your breathing, posture, the way you walk, a certain touch, and messages that remind you to stay in a calm, focused, energetic, at-ease and centered state during tense and uncomfortable situations. These cues and others can operate as *anchors* for your Relaxed Core State.

The following list provides some examples of Relaxation Anchors which you can use to remind yourself to stay calm and relaxed. From these, select the ones that you want to make your own anchors.

Feeling anchors
- Touching your heart
- Opening your right hand
- Pulling your shoulders back while sitting
- Standing up straight
- Holding your hands together
- Walking with your feet parallel

Visual anchors
- Sunset
- Sunrise
- Photographs

Hearing anchors
- Favorite song
- Music
- Sound of the ocean
- Your breath

How do I create my own relaxation anchor?
1. Feel, see, and hear yourself in a situation where you remain calm, centered, focused, energized, and relaxed.

2. In your Relaxed Core State, select two Relaxation Anchors.

Remember, be prepared for a very positive aware life

Sample anchors

Breathing
- Inhale breath, hold to a count of 5 and release.
- Breath Refresher exercise (see p. 12).

Breath Walk In and Out
Walk and hear yourself saying "Breath Coming In and Breath Coming Out" (see p.16).

Posture—sitting anchor
Set this anchor while sitting in your Relaxed Core State.
Place your feet parallel and move your shoulders back (see p. 25).

Posture—standing anchor
Set this anchor while standing in your Relaxed Core State
Place your hands by your sides and access the feeling of "standing up straight" (see pp. 27—28).

Focusing eye anchor
Use your watch as a relaxation anchor (see p. 37).

Affirmation anchor
Opening your mind affirmation (see p. 53).

Visualization anchor
Persistence Pays—Visualization Thought (see p. 60).

Test Out your Relaxation Anchor
1. Feel, see, and hear yourself in a situation where you feel stressed.

2. Release your Relaxation Anchor (open your palms by your side). Test this by asking yourself, "Did releasing my Relaxation Anchor shift my mind and body into a calm and centered state?"

3. Notice if your breathing becomes more relaxed? Does your posture shift you into your Relaxed Core State? How do you feel?

4. Now take a moment and magnify or intensify the feelings you experience while in your Relaxed Core State. Imagine your body becoming larger and more calm. Turn up the volume of your soothing voice in your Relaxed Core State.

5. Release your Relaxation Anchor rapidly fives times. Each time you do this, intensify the feeling it gives you. Feel yourself becoming more calm, centered, and at ease.

When you first start using Relaxation Anchors, release the anchor a few times. This process may take time to integrate into your memory. After some practice, releasing your Relaxation Anchor will become easy. Each time you will feel more alive, vibrant, and energized.

Recapping Day Six

Relaxation Anchors

With the learnings and experiences of Day Six in this program, you have now added more additional tools: **Pattern Interrupts** and **Relaxation Anchors** as reminders to stay in your **Relaxed Core State.** Practice each day connecting to your anchor as you find the resources and signals that stimulate and remind you to feel calm, centered, focused, energetic, at ease. You have probably discovered how easily you can create these anchors by using different parts of your body. We consider any anchor that involves the use of your body as an internal anchor. Now you can create anchors using a wide range of words, sounds, sights, and feelings.

External anchors can range from pictures in your home or office to your favorite songs on the radio. We create internal anchors on (or in) the body which then allow us to feel the association. Internal anchors involve your breathing, posture, the way you walk, and a certain touch. Keep practicing and becoming familiar and comfortable with the location and position of your internal and external anchors. As you keep applying your anchor, stepping into your Relaxed Core State becomes easier and easier.

You have also learned that sometimes, before you can feel a calm, relaxing, and resourceful thought, you have to simply *stop* the current flow of thoughts. **Pattern Interrupts** offer us a process for doing just this. And messages that remind you to stay in a calm, focused, energetic, at ease and centered state during tense and uncomfortable situations can operate as **anchors** for your Relaxed Core State.

You do have a choice. You can interrupt the hurt and the spiraling negative state. Or you can remind yourself to stay relaxed and calm by focusing on your **Posture, Breath, Thoughts, Feelings** and **Language.** When you do this, you interrupt the unproductive anchors in the process.

Day Seven: The Language of Relaxation

Relaxation Language

Relaxation Vocabulary refers to the words and phrases you use to describe situations.

- How would you describe a relaxed and comfortable situation?
- Now describe a stressful situation. Notice the words you use to describe both of these situations.
- Your choice of words and phrases influences your feelings.

As an example, look at yourself in a mirror and say the following words, thinking of something that you did recently, "I failed, I totally failed to reach my ideal." When you complete that, how do you feel having said those words? Note the expression on your face as you said them.

Now look at yourself and say, "I succeeded in some ways, and learned how to respond in a smarter way." With the saying of these words, how do you feel? What does your expression look like? It becomes clear, does it not, that your choice of language does indeed affect your body? You can see that some words and the phrases that you use can move you into your Relaxed Core State while others shift you into a Non-relaxed State.

The following offers a **Three Step Process** designed to take advantage of language in order to improve your perspective on life.

1. See the situation that produces stress. Hear the language you and other people use. Feel how you feel affected by your language and that of others.

2. Replace negative words and phrases with positive, uplifting words and phrases.

3. Repeat to yourself silently, but with a loud internal voice, positive, uplifting words or phrases that you find solution-oriented. See yourself in the mirror. Then, ask yourself how you feel when you use a different set of uplifting words and phrases.

Words and Phrases in Non-relaxed and Relaxed State

Non-relaxed state	Relaxed state
• I'm so stressed.	• What do I need?
• I'm never going to get this done!	• Let me think how I can finish this.
• I'm so frustrated!	• This feels challenging; I wonder how I will handle this in an effective way.
• I can't listen to you now.	• Let's set a time to talk.
• I'm in a rush.	• I can do this another time.
• I can't think.	• Let's create a solution.
• Not now!	• A later time would work better.

Name some words and phrases that you frequently use. See how you feel when you replace positive, uplifting words and phrases.

Non-relaxed state	Relaxed state
Can't, should not, never, won't, will try	Maybe, will have a go, will be open, look for options and choices, expand your picture

Habit-forming Vocabulary

Habit-forming vocabulary involves the words and phrases that you often use to describe your emotions and experiences.

For example, suppose you say, "I feel so unhappy. I can never satisfy my boss." Repetition of these words will continue to bring negative messages to your body. How does this sentence make you feel? What facial expression occurs? How does it affect your breathing? Using negative words will put you into a Non-relaxed State.

Now imagine saying to yourself, "My boss will learn to appreciate me. I always do the best possible job." As you do, let yourself feel how this sentence can shift you into your Relaxed Core State. Be aware of how this sentence makes you feel. How does this sentence sound to you? What facial expression manifests itself now?

Relaxation Metaphors

Relaxation Metaphors paint a picture of how you aspire to become, act, and feel in your Relaxed Core State. Relaxation metaphors use words and phrases that remind you of the way you would like to feel in your Relaxed Core State.

Applying relaxation metaphors is a three-step process:

1. See the situation that produces the feelings of stress.
   Hear the language you and other people use.
   Feel how your language and that of others affects you.
2. Replace negative words and phrases with positive, uplifting words and phrases. The more times you repeat the words and phrases, the stronger your Relaxed Core State becomes.
3. Notice how you feel when you say the new words and phrases to yourself.

Example	
I can't concentrate.	I will allow my mind to become centered and focused.
I feel nervous.	I feel calm and relaxed.
I feel depressed.	I am feeling better all the time.

Brian, a real estate broker, arrived in my (D.L.) office feeling frustrated. His business had fallen into a slow period and he found himself having difficulty expressing himself. We looked at the vocabulary he used. He repeated the words "despair" and "failure" over and over. He kept thinking and filling his mind with these and many other negative thoughts. It became obvious that all of these negative habitually used words made him feel depressed. We practiced using positive words and repeating that the business would soon turn around. He told himself that he did the best job possible and knew that he excelled as a broker.

We also looked at and discussed metaphors he could use to describe his business. Brian began to see the business more in cycles. He just came out of a peak period and realized that some time would now pass before the next peak period. Looking at his field from this new perspective made him feel better. A few weeks later Brian phoned and told me he was doing better than ever.

Recapping Day Seven

Flying into a State of Relaxation

Now that you have had seven days of training in many facets of relaxation, you have all the skills you need in order to *quickly put yourself into an optimal state of relaxation.* Using the two royal roads to state (i.e. mind and body, your neuro-linguistics), you can now use thought and action, linguistics and behavior to quickly step into your Relaxed Core State. You can fly into a calm. You can experience **instant relaxation** whenever you choose.

Will you **act your way** into the relaxed state or will you **think your way** into it? Ultimately, it really does not make any difference which you choose. Each will activate the other given the holistic and interactive mind-body system. We would suggest that you choose whichever choice comes more easily for you. So, which do you find yourself more skilled at? Which seems easier?

The process of "flying into a calm" involves using what you've learned in the past seven days. So, as you allow yourself even now to relax—fully and completely—just do so while observing at the same time how you do this. Do you remember a relaxing time? Do you imagine what a relaxing experience would feel like? Do you see pictures which allow you to then take a deep breath and relax?

When you turn on music that you find calming, do you find yourself breathing more deeply, adjusting your posture, or relaxing your face muscles?

If what you do has the effect of inducing a more and more relaxed state, you are making a good choice. Continue to do that. And as you practice **flying into a calm,** do so with the growing satisfaction and awareness that, every time you do so, you are training your nervous system to become even more proficient and skilled in state management. Also, allow yourself to observe the process, noticing what makes it richer and fuller, more satisfying and empowering, purer and more intense.

Prior to this training, many people could only "fly into a rage." Now they can use the same neurological and linguistic processes to "fly into a calm" or, for that matter, into any other resourceful state that they target.

part 3

personal relaxation plan

Chapter *Three*

*P*ersonal Relaxation Plan

Congratulations! You have made the effort to complete the seven-day program. By now, you should start feeling and noticing a change in yourself. Your Personal Relaxation Plan will reinforce the resources, tools, strategies and techniques which will help you to stay calm, centered, focused, energized and at ease in stressful situations.

The Personal Relaxation Program consists of:

1. The Relaxation Toolbox
   Relaxation Signals
   Anchors
2. Morning Relaxation Routine
   Morning Relaxation Reminders
3. Daily Relaxation Reminders
   Daily Relaxation Bonus Reminders
4. Evening Relaxation Routine
   Evening Journal Questions
5. Creating your Ideal Relaxed Environment
   at Home
   at Work
6. Seven-Day Relaxation Plan
   Morning and Evening Relaxation Exercise Routine
7. Relaxation of Parts

When you complete your Personal Relaxation Plan, you will have completed the steps to Relaxation Mastery. The two main goals are:

1. The ability to reach your Relaxed Core State instantly

and

2. The ability to remain in your Relaxed Core State during stressful situations.

The Relaxation Toolbox

Relaxation Signals

Developing your own relaxation signals will indicate to you those times when you have entered your Relaxed Core State. Use the following elements as your checklist.

RELAXATION CHECKLIST
— **B**reathing and Walking Patterns
— **P**osture check
— while sitting
— while standing
— **F**ocusing patterns
— **A**ffirmations
— **V**isualizations
— **P**attern Interrupts
— **A**nchors
— **L**anguage of Relaxation

Be Prepared For A Very Positive Aware Life!

What situations frequently make you feel focused, centered, calm, energetic and at ease? These situations move you towards your Relaxed Core State.

BREATHING
In my Relaxed Core State, my breath feels like:

_____

_____

BREATH—WALKING
In my Relaxed Core State, I walk like:

_____

_____

POSTURE—SITTING
In my Relaxed Core State, I sit like:

_____

_____

POSTURE—STANDING
In my Relaxed Core State, I stand like:

_____

_____

FOCUSING
In my Relaxed Core State, I use these focusing eye exercise(s):

_____

_____

AFFIRMATIONS
In my Relaxed Core State, I remember these affirmation(s):

_____

_____

VISUALIZATIONS
In my Relaxed Core State, I see these Relaxation Thought(s):

_____

_____

PATTERN INTERRUPTS
These pattern interrupts help me to reach my Relaxed Core State:

_____

_____

Anchors

Stress triggers refer to the situations that cause you the most stress in your life. (20% OF YOUR ACTIONS CAUSE 80% OF YOUR STRESS)

To isolate your stress trigger, ask yourself—
What situations cause you the most stress?

1. _____
_____
_____

2. _____
_____
_____

3. _____
_____
_____

When this situation occurs, how do you want to feel in your Relaxed Core State?
When selecting anchors, choose a part of the exercise which is connected to your Relaxed Core State.
What breathing technique helps you to anchor your Relaxed Core State?
(Create a breath anchor for yourself, See pp. 12—15)
i.e. Feeling my breath move in and out through my nose

_____
_____
_____

What form of breath walking helps you to anchor your Relaxed Core State?
(Create a breath walk anchor for yourself, see pp. 11—20)
i.e. Walking and saying Breath Coming In and Breath Coming Out

_____

_____

_____

What form of sitting posture helps you to anchor your Relaxed Core State?
(Create a posture anchor for yourself, see pp. 25—26)
i.e. Feet parallel and elbows back

_____

_____

_____

What form of standing posture helps you to anchor your Relaxed Core State?
(Create a posture anchor for yourself, see pp. 27—28)
i.e. Head is level

_____

_____

_____

What focused eye movements helps you to anchor your Relaxed Core State?
(Create an eye anchor, see page pp. 33—40)
i.e. Focus on relaxation object (photo in my office)

_____

_____

_____

RELAXATION ANCHOR (see pp. 69—72)
When I do not feel relaxed, I will use these Relaxation Anchors:

Breath Anchor _____

Breath Walking Anchor _____

Posture Anchor (sitting) _____

Posture Anchor (standing) _____

Focused Eye Anchor _____

Toolbox for reaching your Relaxed Core State

LANGUAGE
When I have accessed and entered my Relaxed Core State, I will use the following words in the particular situation I am imagining.

RELAXATION VOCABULARY and LANGUAGE (see pp. 74—76)
When I do not feel relaxed, I will use these words and phrases to help me relax.

_____

_____

RELAXATION METAPHOR (see p. 76)
When I do not feel relaxed, I will use this Relaxation Metaphor:

_____

_____

RELAXATION INTERRUPTS (see pp. 67—69)

When I do not feel relaxed, I will use the following Relaxation Interrupt to help me relax:

e.g. Open my left palm

_____

_____

Morning Relaxation Routine

1. Make a commitment to reach your Relaxed Core State each morning. Write down a situation which may cause you stress today.

    _____

    _____

    Rehearse in your mind the Relaxation Signals you will use: (refer to pp. 70—71)

    _____

    _____

2. Ask yourself Morning Relaxation Questions.
    What happens when you reach your Relaxed Core State first thing in the morning?

    _____

    _____

    What happens when you reach your Relaxed Core State at work?

    _____

    _____

How will your relationship improve with your boss?

_____

_____

How will your day improve?

_____

_____

Who will remind you to reach your Relaxed Core State in stressful situations?

Friends _____

Family _____

At work _____

Work Associates _____

What signals will they use to remind you to reach your Relaxed Core State?

Friends _____

Family _____

Work Associates _____

Morning Relaxation Reminders

Choose these activities to help you relax first thing in the morning.

Each morning play Relaxation Music in the form of tapes, CDs, radio.
Select a tape or CD you will play each morning.
CD or TAPE _____

BE PREPARED FOR A VERY POSITIVE AWARE LIFE EXERCISE.
(see below and circle the affirmations)

I practice the following Breath Affirmation:

_____

I practice the following Posture Affirmations:

_____

I practice the following Focusing Affirmations:

_____

I practice the following Core State Affirmations:

_____

I practice the following Core State Visualizations:

_____

BREATH AFFIRMATIONS

- Deep Hourly Breath
- Quick Breath
- The Relaxing Breath

THE DEEP HOURLY BREATH & AFFIRMATION

"I am aware of my breathing throughout the day."

"At the beginning of each hour, I take ten deep breaths, slowly inhaling and slowly exhaling through my nose."

"I see, hear and feel myself becoming more and more relaxed with each breath that I take."

THE QUICK BREATH & AFFIRMATION

"I start off the beginning and end of each hour with ten quick breaths."
"I quickly inhale and exhale through my nose. This rapid sequence of breathing brings me additional energy."

THE RELAXING BREATH & AFFIRMATION

"My breath helps me to relax."
"As I inhale, I become more relaxed."
"As I exhale, I become even more relaxed."

BREATH WALKING AFFIRMATIONS

- Nose Breathing
- Abdomen Breathing

"When I walk, I remember to breathe in through my nose. I pay attention to my breathing patterns and listen to the sound of my breath."

"At the end of each half-hour, I walk and practice abdomen breathing. I feel my abdomen moving in and out as I breathe."

POSTURE AFFIRMATIONS

- Posture Sitting Check
- Posture Standing Check

Posture Sitting Check

"I notice my posture throughout the day."

"At the beginning of each hour, I check that my posture feels comfortable. I check to make sure that I am sitting in a relaxed position. I check to make sure that I have my back straight, my shoulders pulled back, my chin in the middle, and my neck relaxed."

Posture Standing Check

"At the beginning of each hour, I check that I am standing in a comfortable position. I make sure that I have my feet parallel, that I have my knees slightly bent and my buttocks slightly tightened. I will relax my shoulders and keep my head straight."

Focused eye Affirmations
Eye-focus Affirmation
Eye-clock Affirmation

"When I find myself starting to feel stressed, I practice the four-object focus exercise. As I look at four separate objects for ten seconds, I remind myself to relax." I repeat this sequence for five minutes.

"When I find myself pressed for time or in a rush, I take a minute to look at my watch and practice the relaxed eye-clock exercise. I look at my watch and focus on the 12, 3, 6, 9 and 12." I repeat this sequence for five minutes.

Affirmations
Commitment to the core state and affirmation

1. Commitment to staying Focused, Aware, Centered
2. Commitment to Positive Thoughts

1. I feel committed to mastering the Relaxed Core State. "This represents a state that I achieve when I become calm, centered, focused, energized and at ease. No obstacle or challenge will interfere with my state of relaxation."

2. I have made a promise to myself, a promise to reward myself with a life full of ease, peace, calmness and a relaxed state of being.
   "When I think negative thoughts, I become aware of how I feel affected. Immediately, I think of thoughts that I find positive and uplifting."

Visualization
1. I select one visualization-relaxation thought for the day.
2. Twice, during the day, I will see and imagine this thought. I will feel the effects of my visualization.

Additional Morning Relaxation Reminders

Do you drink coffee, tea or juice in the morning? If so, use this morning ritual as a relaxation anchor. When you have brought your cup of coffee or tea to the office, take a sip and place your cup down.

1. First, visualize yourself in a stressful situation which may occur today. Hear yourself speaking and feel the effects of stress. Write down the situation.

_____

_____

_____

_____

2. Use affirmations to tell yourself that the situation will improve. See and hear yourself and the people in the situation remaining calm. Anchor in this feeling of your Relaxed Core State. (Please write down the affirmation.)

_____

_____

_____

During your day, when you feel a stressful situation about to occur, reach for your cup. Hold the cup in your hand. Take a sip and let the feelings of your Relaxed Core State relax you.

Daily Relaxation Reminders

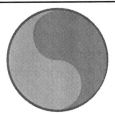

Every day remind yourself to practice Instant Relaxation Exercises.

You can place these Relaxation Reminders in your home:
- Place a note on your bathroom mirror.
- Place a note on your television.
- Place a note on your door.
- Place a note on the inside of your car.
- Leave notes in your filofax.
- Leave yourself a message on the answering machine.
- Every day remind yourself to practice Instant Relaxation Exercises.

You can place these Relaxation Reminders in your home: "I will place three relaxation reminders in my home":

1.

2.

3.

You can paste Relaxation Reminders at work:
- On a Post-it on your telephone.
- On your work calendar.
- On a Post-it on your computer screen.
- On a Post-it on your filing tray.

Every day remind yourself to practice **Instant Relaxation Exercises**: "I will place Relaxation Reminders in the following places at work":

1.

2.

Daily Relaxation Bonus Reminders

- Have three co-workers send you an e-mail as a Relaxation Reminder during different times of the day. The note may say:

"Relax—I want you to take a deep breath."

Then you can place your hands on your desk and slowly count to 5.

Tell yourself to relax after each number.

Example: 1 relax, 2 relax, 3 relax, 4 relax and 5 relax.

The following three co-workers will send me relaxation e-mails. Relaxation Reminders.

1.

2.

3.

Evening Relaxation Routine
Evening Journal Questions

At the end of each day, remember to write in your Relaxation Journal. In this journal, answer four questions. These important questions will help you to see and feel your progress while practicing Instant Relaxation Exercises.

Instant Relaxation Exercises

Start out by selecting a beautiful journal. Find a beautiful picture and paste it on the front of your journal. Do you feel relaxed when you reach for your journal? If so, you selected a photo that works for you. When you feel ready to start this exercise, take a few minutes and write the answer to the following four questions.

Just answer these four questions:

1. How did I help myself to relax today? (How specifically?)
    What did I see, hear and feel?

_____

_____

_____

2. How did I relax during this stressful situation?
    What did I see, hear and feel?

_____

_____

_____

3. What Relaxation Technique did I try today?

_____

_____

_____

4. How did this technique help me to relax?

_____

_____

_____

How did my new, relaxed attitude improve and enhance the quality of my life?

Consider the following areas:
- relationships with your partner, children, parents, work associates, other.

_____

_____

_____

Creating your Ideal Relaxed Environment at Home

Have you ever walked into a friend's home and thought, "This place feels great and smells so fresh." Your friend shows you her house. As she walks you around her home, you see floral arrangements in beautiful vases. You smell beautiful scents. You hear soothing music playing in the background. You say to yourself, "I would love my home to be like this." Or perhaps you have also walked into a store or a restaurant that made you feel great? Did you spend more time in this place because you felt so calm?

Your environment obviously affects your moods. Why not turn one room of your home into a relaxation room? As you step into this room, allow yourself to feel calm, at ease and relaxed. Let's take a few minutes and create your ideal relaxed environment.

Which room(s) of your house will you designate as a relaxation room?

_____

_____

Describe your ideal relaxed environment. How will it look?

_____

_____

How will it sound?

_____

_____

How will you decorate it?

_____

_____

How will it feel?

_____

_____

How will it smell?

_____

_____

Creating your Ideal Relaxed Environment at Work

How do you feel as you walk into your office or workspace? Do you feel energized or do you start to feel lethargic? By adding a few relaxing and soothing touches, you can create a workspace that feels more alive. Let's take a few minutes to create your ideal relaxed environment at work.

What touches will you add to make your work space feel more relaxed?

_____

_____

Describe your ideal relaxed environment at work.
How will it look?

_____

_____

How will it sound?

_____

_____

How will you decorate it? What flowers, trinkets, photos, books will you add?

_____

_____

How will it feel?

_____

_____

How will it smell?

_____

_____

Summary
Seven-day Relaxation Plan

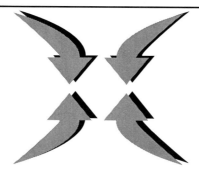

How does it feel having committed to this seven-day Relaxation Plan? After seven days, how much more aware are you of your Relaxed Core State? How much more of an understanding do you have of accessing this part of yourself? Did you notice your Relaxed Core State growing stronger as you practiced Instant Relaxation Exercises? Did you feel the Instant Relaxation Exercises keeping you feeling calm, centered, focused, energized, aware, and at ease as you completed the activities of the day? If you answered "yes" to most of these questions, great. And if not, keep practicing and you will definitely feel the shifts in your body and your mind.

After the first week, remember to keep practicing the same exercises, morning and evening for seven days (five minutes in the morning and five minutes in the evening). Doing this reconditions your body and your mind to continually re-access your Relaxed Core State. Simply practice one exercise from each category. Remove the Instant Relaxation Exercises checklist from the appendix and place it by your bed as a daily reminder to practice these effective, simple and fun exercises.

You will feel so great that you will make this relaxation routine a continual part of your life. We would even recommend that you share this plan with your friends and have your friends or family remind you to keep stepping into your Relaxed Core State. The next time you find yourself in a stressful situation, remember

Be Prepared For A Very Positive Aware Life

and quickly spend five minutes applying the Instant Relaxation Exercises. Smile to yourself as you see, hear and feel the transformational effects of these quick, simple and fun exercises. Notice how you move into your Relaxed Core State, feeling calm, centered, focused, energetic and at ease in the midst of what you once considered a stressful situation.

After you do the exercises, remember to keep a written journal each day. Commit to answering the four relaxation questions for the day. Write your experiences, feelings, beliefs, values and any state changes which come from practicing Instant Relaxation Exercises.

Personal Relaxation Plan

▼ Morning and Evening Relaxation Exercise Routine

In the morning and before going to sleep, practice the following Instant Relaxation Exercises. Select one relaxation exercise from each category.

REMEMBER:

Be Prepared For A Very Positive Aware Life. (Breath, Posture, Focus, Affirmations, Visualizations, Pattern Interrupts, Anchors and Language)

Practice one relaxation exercise from each category.

BREATH EXERCISES
   1. Breath Refresher ❑
   2. Breath Abdomen Refresher ❑

BREATH WALKING EXERCISES
   1. Breath Walk—In and Out ❑
   2. Breath Walk—Abdomen Focus ❑

POSTURE EXERCISES
   1. Relaxed Posture (Sitting) ❑
   2. Relaxed Posture (Standing) ❑

FOCUSED EYE MOVEMENT EXERCISES
   1. Four-Object Eye Focus ❑
   2. Relaxing Eye-Clock ❑
   3. Eye-Letter Connection ❑

AFFIRMATIONS
BREATH
   1. Deep Hourly Breath ❑
   2. Quick Breath ❑
   3. Relaxing Breath ❑

BREATH WALKING
1. Nose Breathing ❏
2. Abdomen Breathing ❏

POSTURE
1. Posture Sitting Check ❏
2. Posture Standing Check ❏

Practice one relaxation exercise from each category

CORE STATE
Commitment to Staying Focused, Aware and Centered ❏
Commitment to Positive Thoughts ❏

AFFIRMATIONS—MIND AFFIRMATIONS
1. Accepting My Mind ❏
2. Changing My Mind ❏
3. Empowering My Mind ❏
4. Energizing My Mind ❏
5. Enjoying My Mind ❏
6. Opening My Mind ❏
7. Protecting My Mind ❏
8. Resting My Mind ❏
9. Strengthening My Mind ❏
10. Thanking My Mind ❏
11. Understanding My Mind ❏

VISUALIZATIONS—RELAXATION THOUGHTS
1. My Past Does Not Equal My Future ❏
2. My Persistence Will Pay Off ❏
3. I Will Improve Every Day ❏
4. I Will Make My Vision a Reality ❏
5. My Life is Always Full of Surprises ❏
6. I Will Just "Go For It" ❏
7. I Will Make a Decision Today ❏

BE PREPARED
When stressful situations arise, have your PAL ready.

PATTERN INTERRUPTS

_____

_____

ANCHORS OF RELAXATION

_____

_____

LANGUAGE OF RELAXATION

_____

_____

You will feel calm, centered, focused, energized and at ease as you learn to relax all parts of yourself. This means that you learn to accept all the different emotions that arise from within you. Some of these emotions include anger, sadness, anxiety, joy, and excitement.

Relaxation of Parts shows you the larger picture of your being. Consider your Relaxed Core State as always there. Most people want to feel calm, centered, focused, energetic, and at ease during their day. You can feel this way even if you find your job stressful. After all, you have many other parts within you: emotions of fear, anger, jealousy, and hatred that co-exist within your being. When you **accept** these parts and **acknowledge** their existence, your mind becomes more restful.

This process involves three steps, which include identifying, acknowledging and accepting all parts of yourself.

In the next seven days, stay in your Relaxed Core State as much as possible.

When you hear yourself talking from your non-relaxed state,

When you hear yourself thinking from your non-relaxed state,

When you see yourself behaving from your non-relaxed state (watch your posture and gestures),

When you feel yourself experiencing emotions from your non-relaxed state,

IDENTIFY
What emotion comes from your non-relaxed part?

_____

What part of you exists in the non-relaxed state?

_____

Relaxation of Parts
Use the IAS technique
(IAS)—IDENTIFY, ACKNOWLEDGE, SELF-ACCEPTANCE

1. Identify the most common emotions you feel in a non-relaxed state (i.e. worry, anxiety, joy, etc.).

The most common emotion that I feel in the Non-relaxed State is:

_____

_____

2. Identify the emotion again and now acknowledge that part of yourself:
   "I acknowledge that_____(emotion) exists within me and operates as a part of me."

3. Now, accept that part of yourself, saying,
   "I accept that_____as a part of myself."
   "This represents the part of me that feels_____."

4. Now exercise unconditional love and acceptance towards that part. Say to it, "I love myself and accept that part of myself that feels_____
_____"

Continue to practice these exercises. You will stay more and more in your Relaxed Core State during your day.

Bob, an organizational consultant, came to me (D.L.) feeling very lethargic. He felt as if he battled between two parts of himself. He felt that in business he had to operate aggressively and yet at home with his wife she expected him to respond to her in a calm and gentle way. Over the years, his wife became upset with his aggressive personality. She even threatened to leave him.

We discussed the theory that Bob had many different sides or parts to his personality. Now he understands that he can leave the aggressive personality at the office. He returns home with that loving part of himself. His wife decided to stay with him and they are much happier.

Conclusion

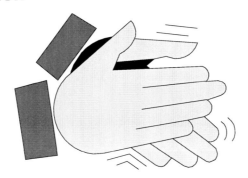

Now, you have completed your Personal Relaxation Plan and have numerous resources, skills, tools and techniques to remain relaxed and empowered in any situation. For the next seven days, continue to practice your favorite exercises from each category.

The categories include:
Breath, Posture, Focus, Affirmations, Visualizations, Pattern Interrupts, Anchors, Language.

Practice five minutes in the morning and five minutes in the evening. Decide that you can allow this routine to become an ongoing process. As you continue practicing, you will keep seeing, hearing and feeling exciting results.

You will become more and more impressed with the changes in your life. During the week, you can remember at numerous times to:

Be Prepared For A Very Positive Aware Life.

This mnemonic offers you a magical phrase that allows you to instantly feel calm, centered, focused, energetic, and at ease. This mnemonic covers many of the non-verbal and verbal aspects of your behavior. Before a tense situation happens, play with **PAL (Pattern Interrupts, Anchors of Relaxation, and the Language of Relaxation). Use breath, posture, focus exercises, affirmations and visualizations to change your state.** Help yourself to feel confident and empowered.

Simply, become more aware of **your breath, your posture, how you walk and your eye movements.** Your **Affirmations** and **Visualizations** will also become constant messages that will assist you in staying in your Relaxed Core State. Notice yourself feeling calmer, more centered, focused, energetic and at ease during your day. Now you have the skills to handle all types of stressful situations.

Allow yourself to use this knowledge to enhance all areas of your life.

Appendix

Personal Relaxation Plan
Instant Relaxation Exercises

▼ **Morning and Evening Relaxation Exercise Routine**

In the morning and before going to sleep, practice the following Instant Relaxation Exercises. Select one relaxation exercise from each category.

REMEMBER:

Be Prepared For A Very Positive Aware Life
(Breath, Posture, Focus, Affirmations, Visualizations,
Pattern Interrupts, Anchors and Language)

Practice one relaxation exercise from each category.

BREATH EXERCISES
    1. Breath Refresher ❑
    2. Breath Abdomen Refresher ❑

BREATH WALKING EXERCISES
    1. Breath Walk—In and Out ❑
    2. Breath Walk—Abdomen Focus ❑

POSTURE EXERCISES
    1. Relaxed Posture (Sitting) ❑
    2. Relaxed Posture (Standing) ❑

FOCUSED EYE MOVEMENT EXERCISES
    1. Four-Object Eye Focus ❑
    2. Relaxing Eye-Clock ❑
    3. Eye-Letter Connection ❑

AFFIRMATIONS
BREATH
    1. Deep Hourly Breath ❑
    2. Quick Breath ❑
    3. Relaxing Breath ❑
BREATH WALKING
    1. Nose Breathing ❑
    2. Abdomen Breathing ❑

POSTURE
    1. Posture Sitting Check ❑
    2. Posture Standing Check ❑

Personal Relaxation Plan—Checklist
Morning and Evening Relaxation Exercise Routine

Practice one relaxation exercise from each category.

CORE STATE
    Commitment to Staying Focused, Aware and Centered   ❏
    Commitment to Positive Thoughts   ❏

AFFIRMATIONS—MIND AFFIRMATIONS
    1. Accepting My Mind   ❏
    2. Changing My Mind   ❏
    3. Empowering My Mind   ❏
    4. Energizing My Mind   ❏
    5. Enjoying My Mind   ❏
    6. Opening My Mind   ❏
    7. Protecting My Mind   ❏
    8. Resting My Mind   ❏
    9. Strengthening My Mind   ❏
    10. Thanking My Mind   ❏
    11. Understanding My Mind   ❏

VISUALIZATIONS—RELAXATION THOUGHTS
    1. My Past Does Not Equal My Future   ❏
    2. My Persistence Will Pay Off   ❏
    3. I Will Improve Every Day   ❏
    4. I Will Make My Vision a Reality   ❏
    5. My Life is Always Full of Surprises   ❏
    6. I Will Just "Go For It"   ❏
    7. I Will Make a Decision Today   ❏

BE PREPARED
When stressful situations arise, have your PAL ready.

PATTERN INTERRUPTS

_____
_____

ANCHORS OF RELAXATION

_____
_____

LANGUAGE OF RELAXATION

_____
_____

Simply, remember:

Be Prepared For A Very Positive Aware Life

Now, you have all the tools and resources to instantly shift you back into your Relaxed Core State—anywhere and anytime!

Bibliography

Bandler, Richard and Grinder, John. (1975). *The Structure Of Magic, Volume I: A Book About Language And Therapy.* Palo Alto, CA: Science & Behavior Books.

Bandler, Richard and Grinder, John. (1976). *The Structure Of Magic, Volume II.* Palo Alto, CA: Science & Behavior Books.

Bandler, Richard and Grinder, John. (1979). *Frogs Into Princes: Neuro-Linguistic Programming.* Moab, UT: Real People Press.

Bandler, Richard and Grinder, John. (1982). *Reframing: Neuro-Linguistic Programming And The Transformation Of Meaning.* Moab, UT: Real People Press.

Bandler, Richard. (1985). *Magic In Action.* Moab, UT: Real People Press.

Bandler, Richard. (1985). *Using Your Brain For A Change: Neuro-Linguistic Programming.* Editors: Connirae and Steve Andreas. Moab, UT: Real People Press.

Bodenhamer, Bobby G.; Hall, L. Michael. (1997). *Time-Lining: Patterns For Adventuring In Time.* Wales, United Kingdom: Anglo American Books.

Dilts, Robert (1990). *Changing Belief Systems With NLP.* Cupertino, CA: Meta Publications.

Hall, L. Michael (1995). *Meta-States: A Domain Of logical Levels, Self-reflexive Consciousness In Human States Of Consciousness.* Grand Jct. CO: E.T. Publications.

Hall, L. Michael. (1996). *Languaging: The Linguistics Of* Psychotherapy. Grand Jct. CO: E.T. Publications.

Hall, L. Michael (1996). *Dragon Slaying: Dragons To Princes.* Grand Jct. CO: E.T. Publications.

Hall, L. Michael (1996). *The Spirit Of NLP: The Process, Meaning, And Criteria For Mastering NLP.* Wales, United Kingdom: Anglo American Books.

Hall, L. Michael; Bodenhamer, Bobby G. (1997). *Figuring Out People: Design Engineering With Meta-programs.* Wales, United Kingdom: Crown House Publishing.

Hall, L. Michael; Bodenhamer, Bobby G. (1997). *Mind-Lines: Lines For Changing Minds.* Grand Jct. CO: E.T. Publications.

Hall, L. Michael. (1998). *Secrets Of Magic: Communicational Excellence For The 21st Century.* Wales, United Kingdom: Crown House Publishing.

Korzybski, Alfred. (1941/1994). *Science And Sanity: An Introduction To Non-Aristotelian Systems And General Semantics,* (4th. ed. & 5th. ed.). Lakeville, CN: International Non-Aristotelian Library Publishing Co.

Instant Relaxation—How To Reduce Stress At Work, At Home And In Your Daily Life, I have shared the resources which most quickly brings you into your Relaxed Core State. These short, easy and fun exercises have been used by people of all ages working in all types of jobs. Testimonials and feedback from my clients reassure me that these exercises are powerful and transformational and the results are long-lasting. Making this Instant Relaxation routine a part of your daily life assures that you have the tools, strategies and techniques to stay relaxed in the midst of chaotic and stressful situations. Imagine not spending any money and being able to control your state—anytime and anywhere. This is an investment in yourself that just keeps growing.

I am extending a personal invitation for you to join **Club Relaxation** at no cost. You will be kept updated by newsletter on the latest advances in stress reduction and mind/body integration techniques. You will also receive information on our other work-books, audio-cassettes, and videos on stress reduction and relaxation programs. Simply send your name, address, and telephone number and e-mail address to the address below for a copy of our catalogue and monthly update of our newsletter.

Debra Lederer
c/o Health Works
422 E. 72nd St, Suite 15D
New York, NY 10021
United States of America
(212) 714-8128
healthws@aol.com
www.balancedyoga.com

Invite your friends and family to join you in practicing these exercises. This will give you a fun and effective way to continue practicing Instant Relaxation Exercises. Start feeling the effects of living life in a much more calm, focused, centered, energetic state.

I invite you to share your experiences with these short, easy and fun exercises. Please send me your stories. I am most interested in your achievement of your Relaxed Core State and wish you fun and blessings along the way.

Best regards,

Debra Lederer

Debra Lederer and Michael Hall, Ph.D. conduct a broad range of trainings integrating the principles and skills that you have read about in *Instant Relaxation*. For a detailed catalogue that includes trainings in Stress Reduction, State Management Skills, Meta-States for Accessing Your Personal Genius, Defusing Hotheads, Communication Enrichment, Meta-Selling, etc, write to:

The Institute of Neuro-Semantics
P.O. Box 9231,
Grand Junction,
CO 81501,
United States of America.
(970) 523-7877
nlpmetastates@onlinecol.com

Both Lederer and Hall custom-design trainings for businesses and organizations.

Still – in the Storm

How To Manage Your Stress And Achieve Balance In Life

Dr Ann Williamson

Why use this particular book to beat stress? Simple. This guide has been designed to be completely useable and accessible, while presenting a programme of exercises that will offer *long-term* stress solutions. It identifies and explains the most empowering, enjoyable and effective stress-relieving techniques, that include:

- hypnosis
- visualisation
- relaxation
- goal setting
- cognitive strategy
- time management
- exercise
- positive mental rehearsal.

Accessibility is the key quality of this book – hence the clarity of its layout, its amusing cartoon illustrations and its reader-friendly tone. But as fun as it is, this book also offers a serious message and comes with the weighty assurance of its author's expertise: Dr Ann Williamson has no less than twenty-five years' experience of helping people handle anxiety. It explains *exactly why* we act and feel the way we do and helps identify *realistic and achievable* goals. It is an attractive and inviting book which offers readers **concrete advice, tried and tested techniques and the latest, most effective exercises in stress management.**

Paperback   80 pages   UK £5.99   USA $8.95   1899836411

Bliss

Coach Yourself to Feel Great

Amanda Lowe

At last! A direct, funny, engaging and colourful book on a subject
that is dear to all our hearts. This book gives many insights into
ways of achieving bliss and is written in a down-to-earth, pragmatic,
conversational style.

Life isn't about how far you can go, how high you can jump and how
much money you can earn. It is about recognising those feelings of bliss
that happen to real people in the real world every day and using those
feelings to bring bliss into every part of your life.

If you've ever felt let down by a self-help book, or couldn't live up to
the rigours of a personal development course, this is the book for you.
Bliss might not change your life, make you popular with the opposite
sex or promise you unlimited success but it will make you laugh, make
you think and open you up to experience bliss whenever and however
you want.

"If there's one book to buy this year, this is it"
Prima Magazine

Paperback   272 pages   UK £9.99   USA $14.95   190442418X

USA, Canada & Mexico orders to:
Crown House Publishing Company LLC
4 Berkeley Street, 1st Floor, Norwalk, CT 06850, USA
Tel: +1 203 852 9504, Fax: +1 203 852 9619
E-mail: info@CHPUS.com
www.CHPUS.com

UK, Europe & Rest of World orders to:
The Anglo American Book Company Ltd.
Crown Buildings, Bancyfelin, Carmarthen, Wales SA33 5ND
Tel: +44 (0)1267 211880/211886, Fax: +44 (0)1267 211882
E-mail: books@anglo-american.co.uk
www.anglo-american.co.uk

Australasia orders to:
Footprint Books Pty Ltd.
Unit 4/92A Mona Vale Road, Mona Vale NSW 2103, Australia
Tel: +61 (0) 2 9997 3973, Fax: +61 (0) 2 9997 3185
E-mail: info@footprint.com.au
www.footprint.com.au

Singapore orders to:
Publishers Marketing Services Pte Ltd.
10-C Jalan Ampas #07-01
Ho Seng Lee Flatted Warehouse, Singapore 329513
Tel: +65 6256 5166, Fax: +65 6253 0008
E-mail: info@pms.com.sg
www.pms.com.sg

Malaysia orders to:
Publishers Marketing Services Pte Ltd
Unit 509, Block E, Phileo Damansara 1, Jalan 16/11
46350 Petaling Jaya, Selangor, Malaysia
Tel : +03 7955 3588, Fax : +03 7955 3017
E-mail: pmsmal@streamyx.com
www.pms.com.sg

South Africa orders to:
Everybody's Books CC
PO Box 201321, Durban North, 4016, RSA
Tel: +27 (0) 31 569 2229, Fax: +27 (0) 31 569 2234
E-mail: warren@ebbooks.co.za